PENGUIN CLASSICS

THE EPIGRAMS

MARCUS VALERIUS MARTIALIS was born c. 40 A.D. in Spain but left there at the age of twenty-three to live in Rome where he came into contact with all classes, from emperor and court downwards. During his thirty-five years in Roman society, he made friends with Juvenal, Quintilian and the younger Pliny and was an extremely keen observer of contemporary life. He published twelve books of epigrams before he finally retired to Spain where he died c. 104 A.D.

JAMES MICHIE was born in 1927 and educated at Marlborough and Trinity College, Oxford, where he read Classics. He is at present a director of the Bodley Head. His publications include a book of poems, *Possible Laughter*, and translations of *The Odes of Horace* and *The Poems of Catullus*.

MARTIAL:
THE EPIGRAMS

*

Selected and translated by
James Michie

PENGUIN BOOKS

PENGUIN BOOKS

Published by the Penguin Group
27 Wrights Lane, London W8 5TZ, England
Viking Penguin Inc., 40 West 23rd Street, New York, New York 10010, USA
Penguin Books Australia Ltd, Ringwood, Victoria, Australia
Penguin Books Canada Ltd, 2801 John Street, Markham, Ontario, Canada L3R 1B4
Penguin Books (NZ) Ltd, 182–190 Wairau Road, Auckland 10, New Zealand

Penguin Books Ltd, Registered Offices: Harmondsworth, Middlesex, England

This translation first published by Hart-Davis, MacGibbon Ltd 1973
Published in Penguin Books 1978
3 5 7 9 10 8 6 4

Translation and notes copyright © James Michie, 1973, 1978
Introduction copyright © Peter Howell, 1973
All rights reserved

Printed and bound in Great Britain by
Cox & Wyman Ltd, Reading
Set in Monotype Scotch Roman

For Francis Huxley

And then what proper person can be partial
To all those nauseous epigrams of Martial?

Byron: *Don Juan*

CONTENTS

TRANSLATOR'S NOTE

THIS selection, which amounts to about a tenth of what he wrote, is not intended to represent 'the best of Martial', although much of the best is in it: the criteria for inclusion were modernity, variety, and, perforce, translatability. Martial arranged his Books so that the seemingly haphazard order of the poems should reflect the odd juxtapositions of life itself. A scatological squib follows a deeply felt epitaph, a sincere tribute to a friend comes next to a contrived panegyric of Domitian. Though his brilliant compression of language is dimmed by translation, the vividness of his picture of Rome towards the end of the first century remains gloriously unobscured. One sees, hears, smells the city – its shops, amphitheatres, lawcourts, lavatories, temples, schools, tenements, gardens, taverns, and public baths, its dusty or muddy streets filled with traffic, religious processions, and never-ending business, its slaves, millionaires, prostitutes, philosophers, quacks, bores, touts, dinner-cadgers, fortune-hunters, poetasters, politicians, and layabouts. In a society supported by slave labour and provided with free bread and entertainment at the Emperor's expense, Martial was one of the privileged citizens who preferred to 'get by' without a regular profession and who were prepared to put up with the nuisance of attending a rich patron in the early morning for the sake of the client's uncertain rewards. He led this life for thirty-five years before retiring to his native Spain, but despite the prevailing note of disgust in his work (an epigrammatist has to appear to be angry) one senses a great capacity for fun and for friendship, and an evergreen curiosity about people. Imperial Rome was probably the first city men felt a periodic need to escape from. The Roman citizen with his 'getaway' villa is the direct ancestor of today's uneasy commuter. Dependent on the financial, social, and sexual amenities of the capital, but always nostalgic for the countryside, Martial was one of the first poets to celebrate, with mixed feelings, the modern megalopolis.

The text is that of the Oxford University Press edition, edited by W. M. Lindsay, except for three alternative readings which I have preferred: Book Four, LXIV, line 4 – 'imminent' for 'eminent'; Book Six, LI, line 4 – 'inquis' for 'inquit'; Book Eleven, XCIX, line 6 – 'nimias' for 'Minyas'.

My thanks are due to Peter Howell and J. P. V. D. Balsdon (whose *Life and Leisure in Ancient Rome* is an invaluable background book) for helpful criticism.

J. M.

INTRODUCTION

MARCUS VALERIUS MARTIALIS, known familiarly in English as 'Martial', was born, somewhere around the year 40 A.D., at Bilbilis, a town which stood high on a hill above the river Salo (Jalón) in the north-east of Spain, not far from Saragossa. He was given the cognomen Martialis because he was born on 1 March. His parents were called Fronto and Flaccilla; of their origins and circumstances we know nothing, but Martial speaks of himself as a real Spaniard, with stubborn hair and bristly legs and cheeks. Under the early Empire Spain, already thoroughly Romanized, enjoyed peace and prosperity. The excellence of education available in the province is demonstrated by the number of writers of Spanish origin who achieved distinction in Rome in the first century A.D. – the two Senecas, father and son, the latter's nephew Lucan, Columella, and Quintilian, to name only the best-known. In about 64 A.D. (during the reign of Nero), Martial took the obvious course for a gifted young man from the provinces, and went to Rome.

His earliest surviving work that we possess is the so-called *Liber Spectaculorum*, written to celebrate the opening of the Flavian Ampitheatre (the Colosseum) in 80. About his life during the previous fifteen or so years we can only speculate. Probably he devoted himself to literary and social pursuits, relying for his livelihood entirely on what he could get from patrons. There is reason to believe that when he first arrived in Rome he benefited from the conspicuous generosity of his compatriot, the younger Seneca, and other members of his family and circle, including the blue-blooded C. Calpurnius Piso. However, in 65 Seneca was involved in a conspiracy to assassinate Nero and substitute Piso as emperor, and the failure of this plot and the subsequent deaths of almost the whole group will have deprived Martial of this source of patronage.

All the same, his wit and talent must soon have found him other patrons. His unwillingness to take up a profession was a matter of choice and not necessity. There is a widespread notion that men like Martial and Juvenal were helpless victims, trapped in a social system which made it impossible for middle-class, well-educated men to earn a living by respectable means, and forced them to live as dependants on the mean and contemptuous rich. This picture is false – although deliberately fostered by Martial and Juvenal themselves. The standard education was largely rhetorical: this meant that any educated man was equipped to plead cases in the courts, or, if not suited to that, at any rate to teach rhetoric. Under the Republic it had been illegal for an advocate to be paid for his services, but by the early Empire, although still not regarded as really good form, and limited by law, it was normal for lawyers to make a reasonable or even handsome living. It is highly unlikely that Martial (or for that matter Juvenal) ever practised in the courts. The reason was simply disinclination. Friends urged him to do so, including even the great Quintilian. He preferred a quiet life devoted to poetry and friendship.

In his earlier years at Rome at least, however, his life cannot have been as quiet as he might have wished. For the disadvantage of living as a 'client' of rich patrons was that it entailed certain services. The relationship between patrons and clients is not easy for us to make sense of. Originally clients were foreigners under the protection of Roman citizens. But by the early Empire they might also be free Romans. Clientship was an informal relationship, governed by custom and not law. The client acquired protection (for instance in lawsuits) and social assistance (such as dinners), while the patron could claim the client's support on those occasions when he felt his status required a numerous entourage – for instance in the law courts, at elections, at literary recitations, or even in his own dining

room. By Martial's time a client seems to have been
expected to call to greet his patron in the early morning,
and accompany him on his social or business round,
receiving at the end a small money 'dole', or, if he was
lucky, an invitation to dinner. He might also receive
occasional presents. All this could, of course, be very
tedious and time-consuming. The client was expected to
wear his toga – hot and sweaty in summer; he might have
to walk long distances through crowded and muddy streets,
up and down the hills of Rome, to reach his patron's house,
and then most of the day might be wasted in trailing
around from one boring occupation to another. In fact,
the number of men who actually depended on clientship
for a living must have been small, and there is evidence to
suggest that, apart from a few literary men like Martial
and Juvenal (who can be suspected of satirically exagger-
ating the whole business), they were mostly idle parasites
and layabouts. The patrons deserve sympathy as well as
the clients.

Martial, of course, had a special means of winning favour
with patrons – by flattering them in his poems. This does
not appeal to modern tastes, and certainly some of his
patrons seem dubious choices – for example, the unscrupu-
lous ex-informer Regulus (V 10; VII 16). We have always
to beware of taking him too seriously – for example, in the
poem where he tells a man whom he has flattered, but who
has failed to reward him, that he has cheated him. Such
rewards were virtually the only way to make money out
of literature. In the absence of copyright, there could be
no question of authors' royalties. There is, however, some
evidence to suggest that when an author became really
well-known, as Martial was by the time he published his
Book I, a bookseller might pay him for the right to be the
first to get his manuscript for copying. This is probably
why Martial, in the first book, recommends the two book-
sellers, Secundus (I 2) and Atrectus (I 117), even giving
their addresses.

It may well be wondered how, at the beginning of his

'*Book I*', an author can describe himself as 'known the world over for his neat and witty epigrams'. In fact *Book I* was not published until about 85, and we know that Martial had written a good deal previously. The only surviving works are the *Liber Spectaculorum* and the two books of couplets written to be sent along with various sorts of gifts (misleadingly known as *Book XIII* and *Book XIV*). But in *Book I* he refers to youthful works which are on sale. '*Book I*' was, in any case, an arbitrary, if significant choice – like a composer's 'Opus I' – for his first really mature work. As regards his worldwide fame, he himself speaks of being read in Gaul, on the lower Danube, in southern Germany, and in Britain.

The reasons for his success are obvious. His poems are short and readable, sometimes entertaining, sometimes serious, and always completely unpretentious. This was rare in his time, when poetry was only too commonly artificial, long-winded, and overwrought, and often dealt with stale mythological subjects. Long epics in imitation of Homer had been declared a mistake by the greatest of the Hellenistic poets, Callimachus: he insisted on brevity and fine craftsmanship. The success of Virgil's *Aeneid*, however, had led to the vapid epics of Valerius Flaccus, Statius, and Silius Italicus. Martial set himself resolutely against this trend, showing himself a true disciple of Callimachus – whom he himself claims to be the greatest Greek epigrammatist. Perhaps the chief single influence on him was Catullus (many of whose poems can justifiably be called epigrams): his dearest wish, he claims, would be to be placed second to Catullus.

The epigram already had a long history by the time of Callimachus. As its name implies, it was originally a poem inscribed on an object such as a funeral monument, a dedication, or a prize. Soon the form came to be used for a wide variety of subjects, including the humorous and erotic. The metre was usually, but by no means exclusively, the elegiac couplet (the vast majority of Martial's poems are in this metre). Under the early Empire the satirical

epigram was much cultivated by Greeks writing at Rome,
though their literary level was low. Martial, however, was
so successful with this type that, chiefly owing to his
example, 'epigram' even came eventually to mean 'short
poem ending in witty turn of thought' (*Concise Oxford
Dictionary*). In fact, Martial drew on the whole of the
earlier tradition and, concentrating on the epigram (in its
widest definition) as his one form of literary expression,
brought it to a pitch of technical perfection never after-
wards rivalled.

He countered the inherent problems of shortness
principally by taking great pains over arranging the poems
in books, so that they varied (or occasionally interrelated)
according to length, metre, and subject-matter. But this
aspect of his art no selection from his works can reproduce.

As Martial himself says, he does not write about gorgons
or harpies: mankind is his concern. It is his acute percep-
tion of human nature, and boundless interest in the life
around him, that makes him so permanently interesting.
But his concern with mankind is not malicious. He is
careful to make this absolutely clear in the Preface to
Book I, where he states categorically that he has not
satirized any real people, not even under fictitious names.
Admittedly, under the early Empire, he would have been
ill-advised to attack people of any importance, for
emperors tended to discourage personal attacks. But
Martial's warm-hearted character would in any case have
avoided spitefulness. As a result, his verse may have lost
some spice for his contemporaries, but it has gained time-
lessness and universality.

The other topic he mentions in his Preface is obscenity.
Here his defence rests chiefly on an appeal to tradition
(citing Catullus among others), and on the familiar argu-
ment that those who don't like it needn't read it (see also
III 86): in I 4 he (like Ovid and Catullus) makes the con-
ventional claim that, although his verse may be loose, his
life is pure. The supposedly scarifying obscenity of the
'nauseous epigrams of Martial' (Byron's facetious epithet)

has unduly affected his reputation. In fact, only a comparatively small proportion of his poems could offend even the most prudish, and they go no further than much of Aristophanes, Catullus, or Juvenal. Modern readers, at least, are unlikely to be disturbed. More positively, he gives us a fascinating insight into an aspect of Roman life on which we have little information. The attitude towards sex that emerges from Martial is one of cheerful permissiveness, but certainly not wild and orgiastic promiscuity. Fornication is acceptable, and prostitution widespread; adultery is technically forbidden, but not to be taken too seriously. Homosexuality (or bisexuality) is regarded as natural, particularly with adolescent partners. 'Perversions' such as oral sex are practised, but not considered quite decent: at any rate, as in the case of homosexuality, the active role is thought comparatively shameless, the passive role definitely shameful. Martial only mentions forms of multiple intercourse once, and then professes horror at them.

It is clear that Martial never married – in spite of poems such as XI 104 where he writes in the person of a husband (when he uses the first person he is not necessarily being autobiographical). He was, however, granted the privileges accorded to a father of three children (introduced by Augustus as a means of raising the birth-rate) by both Titus and Domitian. This was by no means the only way in which he benefited from imperial generosity. It may also have been Titus who gave him the (again titular) military office of tribune, which brought with it the status of a member of the equestrian class (second in rank to the senators). Domitian – who favoured Martial highly – has acquired the reputation of a Hitler, largely as a result of the picture presented by Tacitus, Juvenal, and other biased writers. In fact, for all but disaffected members of the senatorial class, against whom he waged a paranoiac vendetta, his reign was calm and prosperous, marked by beneficial social and moral legislation. The absurd notion – current then as now – that the first century A.D. was a period of 'decadence', with the Roman Empire already careering headlong towards its fall, is answered by Martial himself, at IX 70. Martial's flattery of Domitian may seem gross to us (for example, the frequent comparisons, if not identifications, with Jupiter), and his abuse of him after his assassination is indefensible, though it is hard to blame him for knowing on which side his bread was buttered.

Whether through imperial or private generosity, Martial's material circumstances gradually became more and more comfortable. In the first book (I 117) he lives up three flights of stairs – in other words, in one of those tall and crowded blocks of flats which housed most of imperial Rome. Life in such flats was not very pleasant: there was no running water, or possibility of an open fire for warmth or cooking, and windows were closed by wooden shutters or canvas. For most people, a flat was probably just a place for sleeping (or trying to sleep – not easy, particularly since wheeled traffic was only allowed into the city at night) and keeping goods. Most of life would be led among the plentiful amenities supplied by either private enterprise or public generosity: the numerous eating-houses and taverns, gardens surrounded by colonnades, public lavatories (one at least centrally heated), and, above all, the bath establishments – of crucial importance to the Romans, who bathed every day, and for whom bath-time (before dinner) was an occasion not just for hygiene but for exercise, sociability, and even for more dubious pleasures (see e.g. I 96; IX 33). The great imperial baths were open free, but many preferred the smaller private baths which charged a small entrance fee. The pleasures of the city also included frequent chariot-races and gladiatorial shows.

Eventually – before 94 A.D. – Martial was able to exchange his flat for a small house of his own. He had already possessed a small country estate at Nomentum (Mentana), twenty miles north-east of Rome, for about ten years. He also tells us that he owned a pair of mules (VIII 61), and mentions several slaves (e.g. V 34). However, he still found life at Rome irksome, and its social duties interfered with his writing (X 74; IX 24). Finally he decided to leave. He had already, in about 87, gone off for a stay at Forum Cornelii (Imola, between Bologna and Ravenna). But in 98 (or soon after), after 34 years in Rome, he made up his mind to return for good to his beloved birthplace. The younger Pliny gave him some money to help him on his journey. At first he found life back in Bilbilis idyllic, not least because he had a generous local patron, a lady named Marcella (XII 31). He wrote a rapturous poem to his friend Juvenal, teasing him about the tedious client's life he still lived at Rome (XII 18) – the comparison with Juvenal's famous attack on life at Rome in his third satire (the one adapted by Johnson for his 'London') is intriguing. But before long he grew bored with provincial life – with people pestering him for help (XII 68), small-town scandalmongering, and finding nothing to write about. In any case, although he was well able to appreciate the pleasures of country life (e.g. III 58; IV 66), the truest expression of his ideal existence is to be found in V 20, addressed to his closest friend, Julius Martialis – it is a catalogue of urban delights. An occasional break in the country was enough for him.

Within a few years of his return to Bilbilis (certainly by 104) he was dead. His death was mourned by Pliny (*Epistles* III 21), who paid tribute to his talent, his keen wit, his candour. He doubted, however, if Martial's work would survive. We may be glad that he was wrong. Not only did the poems survive, but their influence on succeeding ages was immense – Juvenal, the late Roman poets, medieval writers, the great crop of Renaissance and Baroque epigrammatists, and many poets of the eighteenth century, were all deeply indebted to them.

PETER HOWELL

LIBER I

I

HIC est quem legis ille, quem requiris,
toto notus in orbe Martialis
argutis epigrammaton libellis:
cui, lector studiose, quod dedisti
viventi decus atque sentienti,
rari post cineres habent poetae.

III

ARGILETANAS mavis habitare tabernas,
   cum tibi, parve liber, scrinia nostra vacent.
nescis, heu, nescis dominae fastidia Romae:
   crede mihi, nimium Martia turba sapit.
maiores nusquam rhonchi: iuvenesque senesque
   et pueri nasum rhinocerotis habent.
audieris cum grande sophos, dum basia iactas,
   ibis ab excusso missus in astra sago.
sed tu ne totiens domini patiare lituras
   neve notet lusus tristis harundo tuos,
aetherias, lascive, cupis volitare per auras:
   i, fuge; sed poteras tutior esse domi.

BOOK ONE

I

May I present myself – the man
You read, admire and long to meet,
Known the world over for his neat
And witty epigrams? The name
Is Martial. Thank you, earnest fan,
For having granted me the fame
Seldom enjoyed by a dead poet
While I'm alive and here to know it.

3

Frail book, although there's room for you to stay
Snug on my shelves, you'd rather fly away
To the bookshops and be published. How I pity
Your ignorance of this supercilious city!
Believe me, little one, our know-all crowd
Is hard to please. Nobody sneers as loud
As a Roman: old or young, even newly-born,
He turns his nose up like a rhino horn.
As soon as one hears the deafening 'bravos!'
And begins blowing kisses, up one goes
Skywards, tossed in a blanket. And yet you,
Fed up with the interminable 'few',
'Final' revisions of your natural song
By my strict pen, being a wild thing, long
To try your wings and flutter about Rome.
Off you go, then! You're safer, though, at home.

IV

CONTIGERIS nostros, Caesar, si forte libellos,
  terrarum dominum pone supercilium.
consuevere iocos vestri quoque ferre triumphi,
  materiam dictis nec pudet esse ducem.
qua Thymelen spectas derisoremque Latinum,
  illa fronte precor carmina nostra legas.
innocuos censura potest permittere lusus:
  lasciva est nobis pagina, vita proba.

X

PETIT Gemellus nuptias Maronillae
et cupit et instat et precatur et donat.
Adeone pulchra est? Immo foedius nil est.
Quid ergo in illa petitur et placet? Tussit.

XXVII

HESTERNA tibi nocte dixeramus,
quincunces puto post decem peractos,
cenares hodie, Procille, mecum.
tu factam tibi rem statim putasti
et non sobria verba subnotasti
exemplo nimium periculoso:
μισῶ μνάμονα συμπόταν, Procille.

4

Caesar, if you should chance to handle my book,
I hope that you'll relax the frowning look
That rules the world. Soldiers are free to mock
The triumphs of you emperors – there's no shame
In a general being made a laughing-stock.
I beg you, read my verses with the same
Face as you watch Latinus on the stage
Or Thymele the dancer. Harmless wit
You may, as Censor, reasonably permit:
My life is strict, however lax my page.

10

Gemellus wants to marry Maronilla:
He sighs, pleads, pesters, sends a daily present.
Is she a beauty? No, a hideous peasant.
What's the attraction, then? That cough will kill her.

27

Last night, after five pints of wine,
I said, 'Procillus, come and dine
Tomorrow.' You assumed I meant
What I said (a dangerous precedent)
And slyly jotted down a note
Of my drunk offer. Let me quote
A proverb from the Greek: 'I hate
An unforgetful drinking mate'.

XXXIV

INCUSTODITIS et apertis, Lesbia, semper
    liminibus peccas nec tua furta tegis,
et plus spectator quam te delectat adulter
    nec sunt grata tibi gaudia si qua latent.
at meretrix abigit testem veloque seraque
    raraque Submemmi fornice rima patet.
a Chione saltem vel ab Iade disce pudorem:
    abscondunt spurcas et monumenta lupas.
numquid dura tibi nimium censura videtur?
    deprendi veto te, Lesbia, non futui.

XXXVIII

QUEM recitas meus est, o Fidentine, libellus:
    sed male cum recitas, incipit esse tuus.

XLVI

CUM dicis 'Propero, fac si facis,' Hedyle, languet
    protinus et cessat debilitata Venus.
expectare iube: velocius ibo retentus.
    Hedyle, si properas, dic mihi, ne properem.

34

Lesbia, why are your amours
Always conducted behind open, unguarded doors?
Why do you get more excitement out of a voyeur than a
    lover?
Why is pleasure no pleasure when it's under cover?
Whores use a curtain, a bolt or a porter
To bar the public – you won't find many chinks in the red-
    light quarter.
Ask Chione or Ias how to behave:
Even the cheapest tart conceals her business inside a
    monumental grave.
If I seem too hard on you, remember my objection
Is not to fornication but detection.

38

They're mine, but when a fool like you recites
My poems I resign the author's rights.

46

When you say, 'Quick, I'm going to come,'
Hedylus, I go limp and numb.
But ask me to hold back my fire,
And the brake accelerates desire.
Dear boy, if you're in such a hurry,
Tell me to slow up, not to worry.

XLVII

Nuper erat medicus, nunc est vispillo Diaulus:
quod vispillo facit, fecerat et medicus.

LIV

Si quid, Fusce, vacas adhuc amari –
nam sunt hinc tibi, sunt et hinc amici –
unum, si superest, locum rogamus,
nec me, quod tibi sim novus, recuses:
omnes hoc veteres tui fuerunt.
tu tantum inspice qui novus paratur
an possit fieri vetus sodalis.

LXIV

Bella es, novimus, et puella, verum est,
et dives, quis enim potest negare?
sed cum te nimium, Fabulla, laudas,
nec dives neque bella nec puella es.

47

Diaulus, recently physician,
Has set up now as a mortician:
No change, though, in the clients' condition.

54

If you've still room in your affections —
For you have friends in all directions —
For one more, may I occupy
The vacant place? You can't deny
Me this simply because I'm 'new':
All your old chums were once that, too.
Think, Fuscus: might not in the end
The newest prove the oldest friend?

64

That you're young, beautiful and rich,
Fabulla, no one can deny.
But when you praise yourself too much,
None of the epithets apply.

LXXIII

Nullus in urbe fuit tota qui tangere vellet
  uxorem gratis, Caeciliane, tuam,
dum licuit: sed nunc positis custodibus ingens
  turba fututorum est: ingeniosus homo es.

LXXVII

Pulchre valet Charinus et tamen pallet.
parce bibit Charinus et tamen pallet.
bene concoquit Charinus et tamen pallet.
sole utitur Charinus et tamen pallet.
tingit cutem Charinus et tamen pallet.
cunnum Charinus lingit et tamen pallet.

73

When you complaisantly allowed
Any man, free of charge, to lay
Hands on your wife, not one would play.
But now you've posted a house guard
There's an enormous randy crowd.
Caecilianus, you're a card.

77

He's healthy – yet he's deathly pale;
Seldom drinks wine and has a hale
Digestion – but looks white and ill;
Sunbathes, rouges his cheeks – and still
Has a pasty face; licks all the cunts
In Rome – and never blushes once.

LXXXVI

Vicinus meus est manuque tangi
de nostris Novius potest fenestris.
quis non invideat mihi putetque
horis omnibus esse me beatum,
iuncto cui liceat frui sodale?
Tam longe est mihi quam Terentianus,
qui nunc Niliacam regit Syenen.
non convivere, nec videre saltem,
non audire licet, nec urbe tota
quisquam est tam prope tam proculque nobis.
Migrandum est mihi longius vel illi
vicinus Novio vel inquilinus
sit, si quis Novium videre non volt.

LXXXVII

Ne gravis hesterno fragres, Fescennia, vino,
  pastillos Cosmi luxuriosa voras.
ista linunt dentes iantacula, sed nihil opstant,
  extremo ructus cum redit a barathro.
quid quod olet gravius mixtum diapasmate virus
  atque duplex animae longius exit odor?
notas ergo nimis fraudes deprensaque furta
  iam tollas et sis ebria simpliciter.

86

Novius is so close a neighbour, I could stand
At my window and touch him with a hand.
'Lucky you,' you say.
'I envy you being able to enjoy at all hours of the day
The companionship of a true brother.'
Not a bit of it. We couldn't have less to do with each other
If he were Terentianus, Governor of the Lower Nile.
I'm not allowed to dine with him, he won't vouchsafe a
    word or a smile.
There's no one so near and yet so distant in all Rome.
Clearly one of us must find a new home.
If you don't want to see Novius, you should live next door
Or, better still, in the same house, on the same floor.

87

Hoping, Fescennia, to overpower
The reek of last night's drinking, you devour
Cosmus' sweet-scented pastilles by the gross.
But though they give your teeth a whitish gloss
They fail to make your breath any less smelly
When a belch boils from your abyss-like belly.
In fact, blended with lozenges it's much stronger,
It travels farther and it lingers longer.
Give up these stale, transparent tricks. A skunk
Must be itself. Why not just be a drunk?

LXXXIX

GARRIS in aurem semper omnibus, Cinna,
garrire et illud teste quod licet turba.
rides in aurem, quereris, arguis, ploras,
cantas in aurem, iudicas, taces, clamas,
adeoque penitus sedit hic tibi morbus,
ut saepe in aurem, Cinna, Caesarem laudes.

XCVI

SI non molestum est teque non piget, scazon,
nostro rogamus pauca verba Materno
dicas in aurem sic ut audiat solus.
Amator ille tristium lacernarum
et baeticatus atque leucophaeatus,
qui coccinatos non putat viros esse
amethystinasque mulierum vocat vestes,
nativa laudet, habeat et licet semper
fuscos colores, galbinos habet mores.
Rogabit unde suspicer virum mollem.
Una lavamur: aspicit nihil sursum,
sed spectat oculis devorantibus draucos
nec otiosis mentulas videt labris.
Quaeris quis hic sit? Excidit mihi nomen.

89

You're always whispering in one's ear
'Secrets' the world might safely hear.
You crack jokes, grumble, weep, accuse
Your enemies, proclaim your views,
Sing songs and shout and even keep
Quiet in a whisper. It's so deep
A sickness that you seldom raise
Your voice, Cinna, in Caesar's praise.

96

My hobbling metre, if it's not a task
Too onerous for you, not too much to ask,
Go and drop a few words in Maternus' ear
Just loud enough for him alone to hear.
He favours drab, dark cloaks, he has a passion
For wearing Baetic wool and grey; the fashion
For scarlet he calls 'degenerate', 'un-Roman',
And, as for mauve, that's 'only fit for women'.
He's all for 'Nature'; yet, though no one's duller
In dress, his morals sport a different colour.
He may demand the grounds of my suspicion.
We bathe together, and his line of vision
Keeps below waist-level, he devours
Ocularly the boys under the showers,
And his lips twitch at the sight of a luscious member.
Did you ask his name? How odd, I can't remember!

CVII

SAEPE mihi dicis, Luci carissime Iuli,
  'Scribe aliquid magnum: desidiosus homo es.'
Otia da nobis, sed qualia fecerat olim
  Maecenas Flacco Vergilioque suo:
condere victuras temptem per saecula curas
  et nomen flammis eripuisse meum.
in steriles nolunt campos iuga ferre iuvenci:
  pingue solum lassat, sed iuvat ipse labor.

CIX

ISSA est passere nequior Catulli,
Issa est purior osculo columbae,
Issa est blandior omnibus puellis,
Issa est carior Indicis lapillis,
Issa est deliciae catella Publi.
hanc tu, si queritur, loqui putabis;
sentit tristitiamque gaudiumque.
collo nixa cubat capitque somnos,
ut suspiria nulla sentiantur;
et desiderio coacta ventris
gutta pallia non fefellit ulla,
sed blando pede suscitat toroque
deponi monet et rogat levari.
castae tantus inest pudor catellae,
ignorat Venerem; nec invenimus
dignum tam tenera virum puella.
Hanc ne lux rapiat suprema totam,

107

Dear Lucius Julius, you often sigh,
'Write something great – you're a lazy fellow.' Give
Me leisure, all the time Maecenas found
For Horace and his Virgil, and I'll try
To build a masterpiece destined to live
And save my name from ashes. When the ground
Is poor, the ox works listlessly; rich soil
Tires, but there's satisfaction then in toil.

109

Issa is naughtier than Catullus' sparrow, Issa is more
appealing than any girl,
Issa is purer than a dove's kiss, Issa is more precious than
an Indian pearl,
Issa is – to end this catalogue –
Publius' doted-on dog.
When she whines, you'd think it was a human voice;
She knows what it is to grieve and to rejoice.
She lies on her master's lap,
Breathing so softly it's inaudible, and takes her nap.
When the call of nature can't be resisted,
She never lets a drop soil the quilt, but wakes you
charmingly with a paw and asks to be set down and
assisted.
She's so innocent of the facts of life
That we're unable to find a mate for such a delicate little
wife.

picta Publius exprimit tabella,
in qua tam similem videbis Issam,
ut sit tam similis sibi nec ipsa.
Issam denique pone cum tabella:
aut utramque putabis esse veram,
aut utramque putabis esse pictam.

CXVII

Occurris quotiens, Luperce, nobis,
'Vis mittam puerum' subinde dicis,
'cui tradas epigrammaton libellum,
lectum quem tibi protinus remittam?'
Non est quod puerum, Luperce, vexes.
longum est, si velit ad Pirum venire,
et scalis habito tribus sed altis.
quod quaeris propius petas licebit.
Argi nempe soles subire Letum:
contra Caesaris est forum taberna
scriptis postibus hinc et inde totis,
omnis ut cito perlegas poetas.
illinc me pete. Nec roges Atrectum –
hoc nomen dominus gerit tabernae – :

To prevent her last dog-day
Taking her altogether away
Publius has had her picture painted. The likeness is so
    complete
That even Issa herself can't compete.
In fact, put both together and you can't tell which is
    which –
Painting or bitch.

117

Lupercus, whenever you meet me
You instantly greet me
With, 'Is it all right by you if I send
My slave to pick up your book of epigrams? It's only to
    lend:
I'll return it when I've read it.' There's no call
To trouble your boy. It's a long haul
To the Pear-tree district, and my flat
Is up three flights of stairs, steep ones at that.
You can find what you want nearer home. No doubt you
    often go
Down Booksellers' Row.
Well, then, opposite Caesar's Forum there's a shop
With door-posts plastered with advertisements from
    bottom to top,
So that at a glance you can read
The list of available poets. There I am. There's no need
To ask Atrectus (the owner's name) for my scroll:
Before you've said a word he'll whip out of the first or
    second pigeon-hole

de primo dabit alterove nido
rasum pumice purpuraque cultum
denarîs tibi quinque Martialem.
'Tanti non es' ais? Sapis, Luperce.

CXVIII

Cui legisse satis non est epigrammata centum,
    nil illi satis est, Caediciane, mali.

Me,
Pumice-stone-smoothed and purple-wrapped, for five
   denarii.
Do I hear you say, 'You're not worth that expense'?
Lupercus, you've got sense.

118

> Caedicianus, if my reader
> After a hundred epigrams still
> Wants more, then he's a greedy feeder
> Whom no amount of swill can fill.

LIBER II

III

SEXTE, nihil debes, nil debes, Sexte, fatemur.
debet enim, si quis solvere, Sexte, potest.

IX

SCRIPSI, rescripsit nil Naevia, non dabit ergo.
Sed puto quod scripsi legerat: ergo dabit.

XI

QUOD fronte Selium nubila vides, Rufe,
quod ambulator porticum terit seram,
lugubre quiddam quod tacet piger voltus,
quod paene terram nasus indecens tangit,
quod dextra pectus pulsat et comam vellit:
non ille amici fata luget aut fratris,
uterque natus vivit et precor vivat,
salva est et uxor sarcinaeque servique,
nihil colonus vilicusque decoxit.
Maeroris igitur causa quae? Domi cenat.

BOOK TWO

3

Sextus, you keep on saying
You're not in debt. I know.
Without the means of paying
One can't be said to owe.

9

I wrote, she never replied:
That goes on the debit side.
And yet I'm sure she read it:
That I put down as credit.

11

Observing Selius pacing to and fro
And up and down Europa's portico
Late in the day, brow clouded, listless air
Hinting at secret sorrows, grotesque nose
Grazing the ground, hand clutching at his hair
Or pummelling his breast, one might suppose
He'd lost a friend or a brother. But the fact
Is that his sons are flourishing – long life
To both of them! – his property's intact,
His slaves are in good health, likewise his wife,
His tenants pay, his bailiff doesn't cheat.
What's wrong, then? No one's asked him out to eat.

XV

QUOD nulli calicem tuum propinas
humane facis, Horme, non superbe.

XVIII

CAPTO tuam, pudet heu, sed capto, Maxime, cenam,
    tu captas aliam: iam sumus ergo pares.
mane salutatum venio, tu diceris isse
    ante salutatum: iam sumus ergo pares.
sum comes ipse tuus tumidique anteambulo regis,
    tu comes alterius: iam sumus ergo pares.
Esse sat est servum, iam nolo vicarius esse.
    qui rex est regem, Maxime, non habeat.

XX

CARMINA Paulus emit, recitat sua carmina Paulus.
    nam quod emas possis iure vocare tuum.

15

Hormus, it's thoughtful of you, not stuck-up,
Not to drink healths. Who'd risk sharing your cup?

18

I angle for your dinner invitations (oh, the shame
Of doing it, but I do it!). You fish elsewhere. We're the
    same.
I attend your morning levée, and they tell me you're not
    there,
But gone to wait on someone else. We make a proper pair.
I'm your spaniel, I'm the toady to your every pompous
    whim.
You court a richer patron. I dog you and you dog him.
To be a slave is bad enough, but I refuse to be
A flunkey's flunkey, Maximus. My master must be free.

20

He buys up poems for recital
And then as 'author' reads.
Why not? The purchase proves the title.
Our words become his 'deeds'.

XXVI

Quod querulum spirat, quod acerbum Naevia tussit,
  inque tuos mittit sputa subinde sinus,
iam te rem factam, Bithynice, credis habere?
  Erras: blanditur Naevia, non moritur.

XXVII

Laudantem Selium cenae cum retia tendit
  accipe, sive legas sive patronus agas:
'Effecte! graviter! cito! nequiter! euge! beate!
  hoc volui!' 'Facta est iam tibi cena, tace.'

26

Because the old lady gasps for breath
And sprays saliva in your eye
And coughs as if she'd caught her death,
Do you suppose you're home and dry?
Miscalculation! Naevia's trying
To flirt, Bithynicus, not dying.

27

When Selius spreads his nets for an invitation
To dinner, if you're due to plead a cause
In court or give a poetry recitation,
Take him along, he'll furnish your applause:
'Well said!' 'Hear, hear!' 'Bravo!' 'Shrewd point!' 'That's
   good!',
Till you say, 'Shut up now, you've earned your food.'

XXXVI

FLECTERE te nolim, sed nec turbare capillos;
  splendida sit nolo, sordida nolo cutis;
nec tibi mitrarum nec sit tibi barba reorum:
  nolo virum nimium, Pannyche, nolo parum.
nunc sunt crura pilis et sunt tibi pectora saetis
  horrida, sed mens est, Pannyche, volsa tibi.

XXXVIII

QUID mihi reddat ager quaeris, Line, Nomentanus?
  Hoc mihi reddit ager: te, Line, non video.

36

I wouldn't like you with tight curls
Nor yet too tousled. Both a girl's
Complexion and a gipsy's tan
Are unattractive in a man.
Beards, whether Phrygianly short
Or wild like those defendants sport,
Put me off, Pannychus, for I hate
The 'butch' and the effeminate
Equally. As it is, your trouble
Is that despite the virile stubble
That mats your chest and furs your leg
Your mind's as hairless as an egg.

38

You ask me what I get
Out of my country place.
The profit, gross or net,
Is never seeing your face.

XLIV

Emi seu puerum togamve pexam
seu tres, ut puta, quattuorve libras,
Sextus protinus ille fenerator,
quem nostis veterem meum sodalem,
ne quid forte petam timet cavetque,
et secum, sed ut audiam, susurrat:
'Septem milia debeo Secundo,
Phoebo quattuor, undecim Phileto,
et quadrans mihi nullus est in arca.'
O grande ingenium mei sodalis!
durum est, Sexte, negare, cum rogaris,
quanto durius, antequam rogeris!

LV

Vis te, Sexte, coli: volebam amare.
parendum est tibi: quod iubes, colere:
sed si te colo, Sexte, non amabo.

44

The moment I buy three or four pounds of plate,
A new slave or a woollen toga, my mate
Sextus the money-lender, whom I've known
For donkey's years, assumes I want a loan,
Panics and takes precautions. I soon hear
His growled aside (intended for my ear):
'I owe Phoebus four thousand, there's eleven
Due to Philetus, and Secundus's seven . . .
I've nothing in my strong-box left to lend.'
Oh, he's a master of the arts, my friend.
To say no, Sextus, when a pal applies
Is cruel. But before he even tries . . . !

55

I wanted to love you: you prefer
To have me as your courtier.
Well, I must follow your direction.
But goodbye, Sextus, to affection.

LXVII

Occurris quocumque loco mihi, Postume, clamas
  protinus et prima est haec tua vox 'Quid agis?'
hoc, si me decies una conveneris hora,
  dicis: habes puto tu, Postume, nil quod agas.

LXXXII

Abscisa servom quid figis, Pontice, lingua?
  nescis tu populum, quod tacet ille, loqui?

LXXXVII

Dicis amore tui bellas ardere puellas,
  qui faciem sub aqua, Sexte, natantis habes.

67

Whenever, Postumus, you meet me
You rush forward and loudly greet me
With 'How do you do?' Even if we meet
Ten times in an hour you still repeat
'How do you do?' How does one do
As little with one's time as you?

82

Why did you cut out your slave's tongue,
Ponticus, and then have him hung
Crucified? Don't you realize, man,
Though he can't speak, the rest of us can?

87

You claim that lots of pretty women
    Are mad for you. I wonder.
With that puffed face – like a man swimming
    And slowly going under?

LIBER III

IV

Romam vade, liber: si, veneris unde, requiret,
 Aemiliae dices de regione viae.
si, quibus in terris, qua simus in urbe, rogabit,
 Corneli referas me licet esse Foro.
cur absim, quaeret: breviter tu multa fatere:
 'Non poterat vanae taedia ferre togae.'
'Quando venit?' dicet: tu respondeto: 'Poeta
 exierat: veniet, cum citharoedus erit.'

V

Vis commendari sine me cursurus in urbem,
 parve liber, multis, an satis unus erit?
unus erit, mihi crede, satis, cui non eris hospes,
 Iulius, adsiduum nomen in ore meo.
protinus hunc primae quaeres in limine Tectae:
 quos tenuit Daphnis, nunc tenet ille lares.
est illi coniunx, quae te manibusque sinuque
 excipiet, tu vel pulverulentus eas.
hos tu seu pariter sive hanc illumve priorem
 videris, hoc dices 'Marcus havere iubet,'
et satis est: alios commendet epistola: peccat
 qui commendandum se putat esse suis.

BOOK THREE

4

Go, book, to Rome. Asked where you come from, say,
'Somewhere not far from the Aemilian Way.'
If pressed for my address, you may reply,
'Forum Cornelii's the town.' Asked why
I'm not in Rome, state the bald truth: 'He found
The toga'ed client's unrewarding round
Tedious and intolerable.' 'And when,'
Some fool will say, 'does he come back again?'
Tell him, 'He left, a poet. When he can earn
A living on the zither he'll return.'

5

Since, little book, you're bent on leaving home
Without me, do you want, when you reach Rome,
Lots of introductions, or will one suffice?
One will be quite enough, take my advice –
And I don't mean some stranger, but the same
Julius whom you've often heard me name.
Go to the Arcade entrance – right beside it
You'll find his house (Daphnis last occupied it).
He has a wife, who even if you land
Dust-spattered at the door will offer hand
And heart in hospitable welcome. Whether
You see her first, or him, or both together,
All you need say is, 'Marcus Valerius sends
His love.' A formal letter recommends
Strangers to strangers; there's no need with friends.

VII

Centum miselli iam valete quadrantes,
anteambulonis congiarium lassi,
quos dividebat balneator elixus.
quid cogitatis, o fames amicorum?
regis superbi sportulae recesserunt.
'Nihil stropharum est: iam salarium dandum est.'

XII

Unguentum, fateor, bonum dedisti
convivis here, sed nihil scidisti.
Res salsa est bene olere et esurire.
qui non cenat et unguitur, Fabulle,
hic vere mihi mortuus videtur.

XXVII

Numquam me revocas, venias cum saepe vocatus:
   ignosco, nullum si modo, Galle, vocas.
invitas alios: vitium est utriusque. 'Quod?' inquis.
   Et mihi cor non est et tibi, Galle, pudor.

7

Domitian's banned our money dole. Adieu
The worn-out client's pitiful revenue
For being obsequious, which some half-drowned
Superintendent of the bath dealt round.
We've seen the last of 'princely' dividends.
What do you think of the news, my starving friends?
'Let's face the facts,' they say, 'we're on our uppers:
We want a fixed wage, not uncertain suppers.'

12

Last night, Fabullus, I admit,
You gave your guests some exquisite
Perfume – but not one slice of meat.
Ironic contrast: to smell sweet
And yet be desperate to eat.
To be embalmed without being fed
Makes a man feel distinctly dead.

27

Our dinner invitations are one-sided:
When I ask you, you usually come; yet you
Never ask me. I shouldn't mind provided
You asked nobody else. However, you do.
Neither one of us, Gallus, comes out blameless.
What do I mean? I'm stupid and you're shameless.

XXVIII

Auriculam Mario graviter miraris olere.
  Tu facis hoc: garris, Nestor, in auriculam.

XXXVIII

Quae te causa trahit vel quae fiducia Romam,
  Sexte? quid aut speras aut petis inde? refer.
'Causas' inquis 'agam Cicerone disertior ipso
  atque erit in triplici par mihi nemo foro.'
Egit Atestinus causas et Civis – utrumque
  noras – ; sed neutri pensio tota fuit.
'Si nihil hinc veniet, pangentur carmina nobis:
  audieris, dices esse Maronis opus.'
Insanis: omnes gelidis quicumque lacernis
  sunt ibi, Nasones Vergiliosque vides.
'Atria magna colam.' Vix tres aut quattuor ista
  res aluit, pallet cetera turba fame.
'Quid faciam? suade: nam certum est vivere Romae.'
  Si bonus es, casu vivere, Sexte, potes.

28

Marius' earhole smells.
Does that surprise you, Nestor?
The scandal that you tell's
Enough to make it fester.

38

What brings you to the city? What wild scheme,
Sextus, tell me, what money-spinning dream?
'My plan is to become the highest-paid
Pleader in Rome, put Cicero in the shade,
Dazzle the courts in all three Forums . . .' Whoa!
Civis and Atestinus (whom you know)
Were barristers, yet neither managed to earn
Enough for the rent. 'If that fails, I shall turn
Poet: the masterpieces that emerge'll
Convince you that you're listening to pure Virgil.'
You're mad. You see those tramps in threadbare cloaks?
They're all Virgils and Ovids – standing jokes!
'Well, then, I'll haunt rich houses, take the dole.'
Four clients at the most keep body and soul
Together that way; all the rest, pale wraiths,
Starve. 'What shall I do, then? For my faith's
Unshaken: I'll live here.' Honour the gods,
And you may just survive – against the odds.

XLIII

MENTIRIS iuvenem tinctis, Laetine, capillis,
  tam subito corvus, qui modo cycnus eras.
non omnes fallis; scit te Proserpina canum:
  personam capiti detrahet illa tuo.

XLIV

OCCURRIT tibi nemo quod libenter,
quod, quacumque venis, fuga est et ingens
circa te, Ligurine, solitudo,
quid sit, scire cupis? Nimis poeta es.
hoc valde vitium periculosum est.
non tigris catulis citata raptis,
non dipsas medio perusta sole,
nec sic scorpios inprobus timetur.
nam tantos, rogo, quis ferat labores?
et stanti legis et legis sedenti,
currenti legis et legis cacanti.
in thermas fugio: sonas ad aurem.
piscinam peto: non licet natare.
ad cenam propero: tenes euntem.
ad cenam venio: fugas sedentem.
lassus dormio: suscitas iacentem.

43

You've dyed your hair to mimic youth,
Laetinus. Not so long ago
You were a swan; now you're a crow.
You can't fool everyone. One day
Proserpina, who knows the truth,
Will rip that actor's wig away.

44

Why, you ask, whenever you show your face
Is there a public stampede, a vast unpopulated space?
The answer – you may as well know it –
Is that you overact the poet:
A grave fault,
Ligurinus, and one which could easily earn you assault.
The tigress robbed of her young,
The scorpion's tail, the heat-crazed puff-adder's tongue
Are proverbial, but you're worse;
For who can endure ordeal by verse?
You read to me when I'm standing and when I'm sitting,
When I'm running and when I'm shitting.
If I head for the warm baths you make my ears buzz with
    your din,
If I want a cold dip you stop me from getting in,
If I'm hurrying to dinner you detain me in the street,
If I reach the table you rout me out of my seat,
If I drop, exhausted, into bed you drag me to my feet.

Vis, quantum facias mali, videre?
vir iustus, probus, innocens timeris.

XLV

FUGERIT an Phoebus mensas cenamque Thyestae
  ignoro: fugimus nos, Ligurine, tuam.
illa quidem lauta est dapibusque instructa superbis,
  sed nihil omnino te recitante placet.
nolo mihi ponas rhombos mullumve bilibrem
  nec volo boletos, ostrea nolo: tace.

XLVIII

PAUPERIS extruxit cellam, sed vendidit Olus
  praedia: nunc cellam pauperis Olus habet.

XLIX

VEIENTANA mihi misces, ubi Massica potas:
  olfacere haec malo pocula quam bibere.

Do you never pause
To consider the havoc you cause?
You're a decent citizen, upright and pious,
But, by God, you terrify us!

45

Whether or not Apollo fled from the table
Thyestes ate his sons at, I'm unable
To say; what I *can* vouch for is our wish
To escape your dinner parties. Though each dish
Is lavish and superb, the pleasure's nil
Since you recite your poems. To hell with brill,
Mushrooms and two-pound turbots! I don't need
Oysters: give me a host who doesn't read.

48

Olus sold land to build a *pied-à-terre*:
He can't foot bills now, for one foot's in air.

49

You drink the best, yet serve us third-rate wine.
I'd rather sniff your cup than swill from mine.

LV

Quod quacumque venis Cosmum migrare putamus
    et fluere excusso cinnama fusa vitro,
nolo peregrinis placeas tibi, Gellia, nugis.
    scis, puto, posse meum sic bene olere canem.

LVIII

Baiana nostri villa, Basse, Faustini
non otiosis ordinata myrtetis
viduaque platano tonsilique buxeto
ingrata lati spatia detinet campi,
sed rure vero barbaroque laetatur.
hic farta premitur angulo Ceres omni
et multa fragrat testa senibus autumnis;
hic post Novembres imminente iam bruma
seras putator horridus refert uvas.
truces in alta valle mugiunt tauri
vitulusque inermi fronte prurit in pugnam.
vagatur omnis turba sordidae chortis,
argutus anser gemmeique pavones
nomenque debet quae rubentibus pinnis
et picta perdix Numidicaeque guttatae
et impiorum phasiana Colchorum;
Rhodias superbi feminas premunt galli;
sonantque turres plausibus columbarum,

55

Whenever you walk past, Gellia, I can't stop
Myself thinking, 'Cosmus has moved shop':
You reek as if a cinnamon flask had been
Unstoppered and up-ended. Please don't preen
Yourself on bottled charm. Were I to treat
My dog the same way, he'd smell just as sweet.

58

Our friend Faustinus at his Baian place
Doesn't go in, Bassus, for wasted space –
No useless squads of myrtle, no unmated
Planes, no clipped box; true, unsophisticated
Country's his joy. His corners overflow
With tight-packed grain, and jars in a long row
Exhale the breath of autumns long ago.
After November, when the frosts begin,
The rugged pruner brings the last grapes in.
Bulls roar in his coombs, and steers, the nap
Still on their harmless brows, lust for a scrap.
The poultry from the mired yard all roam loose –
Jewelled peacock, speckled partridge, squawking goose,
Guinea-fowl, and the bird that gets the name
Flamingo from its feathering of flame,
And pheasant from unholy Colchis; proud
Cocks tread their Rhodian hens; the cotes are loud
With whirring wings; wood-pigeons coo, wax-pale
Turtle-doves answer; greedy piglets trail

gemit hinc palumbus, inde cereus turtur.
avidi secuntur vilicae sinum porci
matremque plenam mollis agnus expectat.
cingunt serenum lactei focum vernae
et larga festos lucet ad lares silva.
non segnis albo pallet otio caupo,
nec perdit oleum lubricus palaestrita,
sed tendit avidis rete subdolum turdis
tremulave captum linea trahit piscem
aut inpeditam cassibus refert dammam.
exercet hilares facilis hortus urbanos.
et paedagogo non iubente lascivi
parere gaudent vilico capillati,
et delicatus opere fruitur eunuchus.
nec venit inanis rusticus salutator:
fert ille ceris cana cum suis mella
metamque lactis Sassinate de silva;
somniculosos ille porrigit glires,
hic vagientem matris hispidae fetum,
alius coactos non amare capones.
et dona matrum vimine offerunt texto
grandes proborum virgines colonorum.
facto vocatur laetus opere vicinus;
nec avara servat crastinas dapes mensa,
vescuntur omnes ebrioque non novit
satur minister invidere convivae.
At tu sub urbe possides famem mundam
et turre ab alta prospicis meras laurus,
furem Priapo non timente securus;

After the aproned bailiff's wife, and lambs
Queue for the bulging udders of their dams.
Young slaves born on the farm, with skins as white
As milk, sit in a circle round the bright
Fireside, and logs, heaped liberally, blaze
For the domestic gods on holidays.
No butler lolls about indoors whey-faced
With sloth, no wrestling-master's hired to waste
The household oil; there they make use of time
To lure with artfully spread net and lime
The glutton thrush, or play the catch with taut
Rod, or bring home the doe their traps have caught.
The garden's such light sweat to hoe and weed,
The town slaves tend it happily; there's no need
For a nagging overseer – the long-haired,
Mischievous boys are cheerfully prepared,
When the bailiff gives his orders, to obey,
And even the pampered eunuch finds work play.
The country-folk who call never arrive
Without some gift – pale combs straight from the hive,
Somnolent dormice, a cheese pyramid
From Umbria's woods, or capons, or a kid:
The big-boned daughters of the honest peasants
In wicker baskets bring their mothers' presents.
When work is done, the neighbour, a glad guest,
Is asked to dine; no hoarding of the best
Food for tomorrow's feast; all get their fill,
Servers as well; fed slaves feel no ill-will
Waiting on tipplers.
              You, though, who reside
In the suburbs, Bassus, starve in genteel pride:
Your belvedere looks on mere laurel-leaves,
Your garden god is smugly safe from thieves,

et vinitorem farre pascis urbano
pictamque portas otiosus ad villam
holus, ova, pullos, poma, caseum, mustum.
Rus hoc vocari debet, an domus longe?

LX

Cum vocer ad cenam non iam venalis ut ante,
    cur mihi non eadem quae tibi cena datur?
ostrea tu sumis stagno saturata Lucrino,
    sugitur inciso mitulus ore mihi:
sunt tibi boleti, fungos ego sumo suillos:
    res tibi cum rhombo est, at mihi cum sparulo.
aureus inmodicis turtur te clunibus implet,
    ponitur in cavea mortua pica mihi.
cur sine te ceno cum tecum, Pontice, cenem?
    sportula quod non est prosit: edamus idem.

LXIII

Cotile, bellus homo es: dicunt hoc, Cotile, multi.
    audio: sed quid sit, dic mihi, bellus homo?
'Bellus homo est, flexos qui digerit ordine crines,
    balsama qui semper, cinnama semper olet;
cantica qui Nili, qui Gaditana susurrat,
    qui movet in varios bracchia volsa modos;
inter femineas tota qui luce cathedras
    desidet atque aliqua semper in aure sonat,
qui legit hinc illinc missas scribitque tabellas;
    pallia vicini qui refugit cubiti;

You feed your workers city corn, your cheese,
Apples, eggs, wine, fowls, fruit and cabbages
Are carted for you to your frescoed home.
Is this 'the countryside' – or outer Rome?

60

Now I'm no longer a paid client-guest,
Why should I put up with your second-best
Menu when you invite me out? You take
Choice oysters fattened in the Lucrine lake
While I suck whelks and cut my lips. You dine
On mushrooms – I'm given fungus fit for swine.
Turbot for you – for me brill. You enjoy
A splendid plump-arsed turtle-dove – I toy
With a magpie that died caged. Why, Ponticus,
Do we eat with you when you don't eat with us?
The dole's abolished – good: but what's the point
Unless our meat's carved from the same joint?

63

I've often heard you called 'man of the world',
But what does it mean? 'Oh, someone who has curled,
Neatly combed hair and balsam on his skin,
Or cinnamon, who can hum the song just in
From Spain or Egypt, who knows how to prance
And wave his shaved arms to the latest dance,
Who spends the entire day in women's care
Endlessly whispering in an easy chair,
Who reads the notes posted from hand to hand

qui scit quam quis amet, qui per convivia currit,
  Hirpini veteres qui bene novit avos.'
Quid narras? hoc est, hoc est homo, Cotile, bellus?
  res pertricosa est, Cotile, bellus homo.

LXXXVI

Ne legeres partem lascivi, casta, libelli,
  praedixi et monui: tu tamen, ecce, legis.
sed si Panniculum spectas et, casta, Latinum, —
  non sunt haec mimis inprobiora, — lege.

XC

Volt, non volt dare Galla mihi, nec dicere possum,
  quod volt et non volt, quid sibi Galla velit.

And writes them too, who simply cannot stand
His neighbour's arm brushing his cloak, who knows
Who sleeps with whom, who's always asked and goes
To parties, and who's never at a loss
For the full pedigree of a winning "hoss" ...'
Out of your own mouth, Cotilus! Let us say,
'Man of the world' signifies popinjay.

86

Madam, I've warned you many times,
Skip when my book becomes obscene;
Yet you read on. Well, if the mimes
You watch Latinus act on stage
Fail to corrupt you – and I'm clean
Compared with them – then turn the page.

90

She's half-and-half inclined
To sleep with me. No? Yes?
What's in that tiny mind?
Impossible to guess.

LIBER IV

VII

Cur, here quod dederas, hodie, puer Hylle, negasti,
  durus tam subito qui modo mitis eras?
sed iam causaris barbamque annosque pilosque.
  o nox quam longa es quae facis una senem!
quid nos derides? here qui puer, Hylle, fuisti,
  dic nobis, hodie qua ratione vir es?

VIII

Prima salutantes atque altera conterit hora,
  exercet raucos tertia causidicos,
in quintam varios extendit Roma labores,
  sexta quies lassis, septima finis erit,
sufficit in nonam nitidis octava palaestris,
  imperat extructos frangere nona toros:
hora libellorum decuma est, Eupheme, meorum,
  temperat ambrosias cum tua cura dapes
et bonus aetherio laxatur nectare Caesar

BOOK FOUR

7

Hyllus, how can you possibly say
No, when you said yes yesterday?
You used to be so warm; you're colder
Suddenly – why? You proffer airy
Excuses: 'Now I'm that much older,
I've started to shave, I'm getting hairy.'
O long, long single night that can
Turn a young into an old, old man!
Why are you teasing me, contrary
Hyllus? Until today you were
A boy. How did the change occur?

8

The first two hours of the morning tax
Poor clients; during the third advocates wax
Eloquent and hoarse; until the fifth hour ends
The city to her various trades attends;
At six o'clock the weary workers stop
For the siesta; all Rome shuts up shop
At seven; the hour from eight to nine supplies
The oiled wrestlers with their exercise;
The ninth invites us to recline full length,
Denting the cushions. At last comes the tenth.
Euphemus, that's the hour when you prepare
Ambrosia with a major-domo's care
For godlike Caesar who, relaxing, grips
In his great hand the nectar that he sips

ingentique tenet pocula parca manu.
tunc admitte iocos: gressun metire licenti
ad matutinum, nostra Thalia, Iovem?

XXI

NULLOS esse deos, inane caelum
adfirmat Segius: probatque, quod se
factum, dum negat haec, videt beatum.

XXX

BAIANO procul a lacu, monemus,
piscator, fuge, ne nocens recedas.
sacris piscibus hae natantur undae,
qui norunt dominum manumque lambunt
illam, qua nihil est in orbe maius.
quid quod nomen habent et ad magistri
vocem quisque sui venit citatus?
Hoc quondam Libys impius profundo,
dum praedam calamo tremente ducit,
raptis luminibus repente caecus
captum non potuit videre piscem,
et nunc sacrilegos perosus hamos
Baianos sedet ad lacus rogator.
At tu, dum potes, innocens recede
iactis simplicibus cibis in undas,
et pisces venerare delicatos.

Sparingly. Then my jest-books can appear.
Please smooth their passage to the Emperor's ear:
My Muse, shy-footed, dare not importune
Jupiter with her levity before noon.

21

'God doesn't exist, there's no one in the skies,'
Says Segius. If it's justice he denies,
He's right: would he be wealthy otherwise?

30

I warn you, fisherman, for your sake,
Keep well clear of the Baian lake
Or you'll commit a crime. This pool
Is swum in by a sacred school
Of fish who know their master and
Nibble his earth-compelling hand;
What's more, each, being named, will swim,
Called by the Emperor, to him.
Not long ago, by this deep stretch,
Some sacrilegious Libyan wretch
While tugging at his quivering rod
Was instantly struck blind by God
And never saw his catch. Now, hating
His cursèd hooks, he squats here, waiting
For alms. Then, while you still may, go
Hence innocently; but first throw
Some unbarbed morsel in, and wish
Long life to the imperial fish.

XXXIV

SORDIDA cum tibi sit, verum tamen, Attale, dicit,
quisquis te niveam dicit habere togam.

XXXVIII

GALLA, nega: satiatur amor nisi gaudia torquent:
sed noli nimium, Galla, negare diu.

LXIV

IULI iugera pauca Martialis
hortis Hesperidum beatiora
longo Ianiculi iugo recumbunt:
lati collibus imminent recessus
et planus modico tumore vertex
caelo perfruitur sereniore
et curvas nebula tegente valles
solus luce nitet peculiari:
puris leniter admoventur astris
celsae culmina delicata villae.
Hinc septem dominos videre montis
et totam licet aestimare Romam,
Albanos quoque Tusculosque colles
et quodcumque iacet sub urbe frigus,
Fidenas veteres brevesque Rubras,
et quod virgineo cruore gaudet

34

Attalus, you're the butt of a good joke:
His toga's filthy, but he's clean – clean broke.'

38

Galla, say no; for love, unless
It teases, cloys with happiness.
Don't take too long, though, to say yes.

64

My friend's few happy acres vie
With the Hesperides: they lie
On the Janiculum's long spine.
A flat crest with a mild incline,
Un-overlooked his plateau breathes
Serener air, and, when mist wreathes
The valleys, Julius Martial's height
Shines with a private, privileged light.
On starry nights when there's no cloud,
The graceful gable of his proud
Villa lifts gently towards heaven.
From one side you can see the seven
Sovereign hills, a bird's-eye view
Of all Rome, Alba's summits too,
And Tusculum's, and each cool retreat
In the suburbs – old Fidenae, neat

Annae pomiferum nemus Perennae.
Illinc Flaminiae Salariaeque
gestator patet essedo tacente,
ne blando rota sit molesta somno,
quem nec rumpere nauticum celeuma
nec clamor valet helciariorum,
cum sit tam prope Mulvius sacrumque
lapsae per Tiberim volent carinae.
Hoc rus, seu potius domus vocanda est,
commendat dominus: tuam putabis,
tam non invida tamque liberalis,
tam comi patet hospitalitate:
credas Alcinoi pios Penates
aut facti modo divitis Molorchi.
Vos nunc omnia parva qui putatis,
centeno gelidum ligone Tibur
vel Praeneste domate pendulamque
uni dedite Setiam colono,
dum me iudice praeferantur istis
Iuli iugera pauca Martialis.

Little Rubrae, and the goddess' wood
Who likes her annual virgins' blood.
From the other, either road he goes,
North or north-west, the traveller shows
Clear to the eye: the wheels spin round
And yet the carriage makes no sound
To mar sweet sleep; for, though the ridge
Is not far from the Mulvian Bridge
And all the boats that glide and scud
Up and down holy Tiber's flood,
No bargee's shout or bosun's cry
Can climb to vex the ear so high.
This house half out of, half in Rome,
The owner bids you treat as home;
Indeed you'll think of it as yours,
So hospitably are the doors
Opened, the visitor supplied
With every want, nothing denied.
Such liberality once reigned
When King Alcinous entertained
Ulysses, or Molorchus played
Host after Hercules had made
Him rich overnight.
                            You who now call
All but your own grand properties small,
Conscript a hundred men with hoes
To work cool Tibur, or impose
A single manager to run
Setia's vine-terraces as one
Vast farm – I'll still (asking your pardon)
Prefer my namesake's modest garden.

LXVI

EGISTI vitam semper, Line, municipalem,
  qua nihil omnino vilius esse potest.
Idibus et raris togula est excussa Kalendis
  duxit et aestates synthesis una decem.
saltus aprum, campus leporem tibi misit inemptum,
  silva gravis turdos exagitata dedit.
captus flumineo venit de gurgite piscis,
  vina ruber fudit non peregrina cadus.
nec tener Argolica missus de gente minister,
  sed stetit inculti rustica turba foci.
vilica vel duri conpressa est nupta coloni,
  incaluit quotiens saucia vena mero.
nec nocuit tectis ignis nec Sirius agris,
  nec mersa est pelago nec fuit ulla ratis.
subposita est blando numquam tibi tessera talo,
  alea sed parcae sola fuere nuces.
dic ubi sit decies, mater quod avara reliquit.
  Nusquam est: fecisti rem, Line, difficilem.

66

You've spent your whole life in the provinces,
And that's the cheapest way to live there is.
On the odd Ides or Calends you might take
Your dusty toga out and give it a shake;
One dinner-suit lasts you ten summers' wear.
Your scrub and fields offer wild boar and hare
Gratis; you beat your copses and get plump
Thrushes as gifts; fish in abundance jump
Out of your stream, for the asking, on the line;
Your big red jar pours out the next hill's wine.
Your plain hearth's tended by a retinue
Of your own country people – not for you
Some pretty, Greek-born butler. You can screw
Your housekeeper when wine heats up your blood
Or some rough farmer's wife. No fire or flood
Has ever touched your house, no August sun
Ruined your crops, no ship – for you have none –
Gone down at sea. Your solitary vice
Is the good old knucklebones, not desperate dice,
And you stake only nuts. You were the heir
Of a rich, miserly mother, Linus. Where
Are those million sesterces? Since your bereavement
They've vanished. A remarkable achievement!

LXX

Nihil Ammiano praeter aridam restem
moriens reliquit ultimis pater ceris.
fieri putaret posse quis, Marulline,
ut Ammianus mortuum patrem nollet?

LXXI

Quaero diu totam, Safroni Rufe, per urbem,
si qua puella neget: nulla puella negat.
tamquam fas non sit, tamquam sit turpe negare,
tamquam non liceat: nulla puella negat.
Casta igitur nulla est? Sunt castae mille. Quid ergo
casta facit? Non dat, non tamen illa negat.

LXXXI

Epigramma nostrum cum Fabulla legisset
negare nullam quo queror puellarum,
semel rogata bisque terque neglexit
preces amantis. Iam, Fabulla, promitte:
negare iussi, pernegare non iussi.

70

When Ammianus' father breathed
His last, his son, hovering in hope,
Found that the final will bequeathed
Him nothing but a length of rope.
Though none of us dreamed he could regret
The old man's death, he's most upset.

71

Rufus, I've searched all Rome for a long time
To find a girl who says no. There are none.
It seems as if it's simply just not done,
As if it's impermissible, a crime,
To say no. Does that mean that they're all whores,
That virgins don't exist? No, there are scores.
Then what does a good girl do? She doesn't give
Either herself or a plain negative.

81

Now that she's read my epigram – the one
About girls saying no – Fabulla's begun
To be difficult. Already she's thrown back
My first, my second, even my third attack.
Fabulla, do be sensible. When I said,
'Say no' I meant, 'Say the last no in bed.'

LXXXIX

OHE, iam satis est, ohe, libelle,
iam pervenimus usque ad umbilicos.
tu procedere adhuc et ire quaeris,
nec summa potes in schida teneri,
sic tamquam tibi res peracta non sit,
quae prima quoque pagina peracta est.
iam lector queriturque deficitque,
iam librarius hoc et ipse dicit
'Ohe, iam satis est, ohe, libelle.'

89

Whoa, little book! Slow up! Easy there! Steady!
We've reached the finishing post, yet you're still ready
To gallop uncontrollably on, to run
Past the last page, as if your job weren't done.
(I'd have called it a day after page one!)
My reader's fed up now, about to drop,
And my copyist, who longs to shut up shop,
Agrees: 'Whoa, little book! Enough! Full stop!'

LIBER V

IX

Languebam: sed tu comitatus protinus ad me
    venisti centum, Symmache, discipulis.
centum me tetigere manus aquilone gelatae:
    non habui febrem, Symmache, nunc habeo.

X

'Esse quid hoc dicam vivis quod fama negatur
    et sua quod rarus tempora lector amat?'
Hi sunt invidiae nimirum, Regule, mores,
    praeferat antiquos semper ut illa novis.
sic veterem ingrati Pompei quaerimus umbram,
    sic laudant Catuli vilia templa senes,
Ennius est lectus salvo tibi, Roma, Marone;
    et sua riserunt saecula Maeoniden,
rara coronato plausere theatra Menandro,
    norat Nasonem sola Corinna suum.
Vos tamen o nostri ne festinate libelli:
    si post fata venit gloria, non propero.

BOOK FIVE

9

I was unwell. You hurried round, surrounded
By ninety students, Doctor. Ninety chill,
North-wind-chapped hands then pawed and probed and
    pounded.
I was unwell: now I'm extremely ill.

10

'Fame is denied to living authors; few
Readers give their contemporaries their due.
Why is this so?' Well, Regulus, I'll tell you.
The character of envy is to value
The ancients higher than the moderns. So,
Nostalgically, ungratefully, we go
For shade to Pompey's antique colonnade,
So old men praise the ugly temple made
Uglier by Catulus. You read Ennius, Rome,
When Virgil was available nearer home;
In his own century Homer's public found him
Uncouth; Menander's audience seldom crowned him
Or even clapped; though Ovid was a poet,
Corinna was the only one to know it.
But there's no cause, my little books, to worry:
If glory must be posthumous, why hurry?

XVIII

Quod tibi Decembri mense, quo volant mappae
gracilesque ligulae cereique chartaeque
et acuta senibus testa cum Damascenis,
praeter libellos vernulas nihil misi,
fortasse avarus videar aut inhumanus.
odi dolosas munerum et malas artes:
imitantur hamos dona: namque quis nescit
avidum vorata decipi scarum musca?
Quotiens amico diviti nihil donat,
o Quintiane, liberalis est pauper.

XX

Si tecum mihi, care Martialis,
securis liceat frui diebus,
si disponere tempus otiosum
et verae pariter vacare vitae:
nec nos atria nec domos potentum
nec litis tetricas forumque triste
nossemus nec imagines superbas;
sed gestatio, fabulae, libelli,
campus, porticus, umbra, Virgo, thermae,
haec essent loca semper, hi labores.
nunc vivit necuter sibi, bonosque
soles effugere atque abire sentit,

18

Because, this month, when napkins, pretty spoons,
Paper, wax tapers and tall jars of prunes
Fly to and fro, I've sent you nothing but books,
My humble, home-made verses, I may seem
Stingy or impolite. But I abhor
The tricks of the angler's trade. Gifts are like hooks,
And flies, as everyone knows, fool greedy bream.
So, Quintianus, when a man who's poor
Sends nothing to a rich friend, it's an act
Of generosity – in point of tact.

20

If you and I, Julius, old friend,
Were granted licence to expend
Time without worry, infinite leisure,
Together to explore life's pleasure,
We'd neither of us bother then
With the ante-rooms of powerful men,
Arrogant busts, ancestral faces,
Or the law's bitter, tedious cases.
No; strolls, gossip, the Colonnade,
Bookshops, the baths, the garden's shade,
The Aqueduct, the exercise-ground,
Would constitute our onerous round.
But, as it is, we, both and each,
Miss the rich life within our reach.
We watch the good sun speed and set,

qui nobis pereunt et inputantur.
Quisquam vivere cum sciat, moratur?

XXVI

Quod alpha dixi, Corde, paenulatorum
te nuper, aliqua cum iocarer in charta,
si forte bilem movit hic tibi versus,
dicas licebit beta me togatorum.

XXXIV

Hanc tibi, Fronto pater, genetrix Flaccilla, puellam
   oscula commendo deliciasque meas,
parvola ne nigras horrescat Erotion umbras
   oraque Tartarei prodigiosa canis.
inpletura fuit sextae modo frigora brumae,
   vixisset totidem ni minus illa dies.
inter tam veteres ludat lasciva patronos
   et nomen blaeso garriat ore meum.
mollia non rigidus caespes tegat ossa nec illi,
   terra, gravis fueris: non fuit illa tibi.

And the lost day goes down as debt.
Would any man, if he knew how
To live, not do it here and now?

26

In one of my recent literary jokes,
I gave you 'alpha', Cordus, for your cloaks.
By all means, if that poem got your goat,
Award me 'beta' for my overcoat.

34

To you, my parents, I send on
This little girl Erotion,
The slave I loved, that by your side
Her ghost need not be terrified
Of the pitch darkness underground
Or the great jaws of Hades' hound.
This winter she would have completed
Her sixth year had she not been cheated
By just six days. Lisping my name,
May she continue the sweet game
Of childhood happily down there
In two such good, old spirits' care.
Lie lightly on her, turf and dew:
She put so little weight on you.

XXXIX

Supremas tibi triciens in anno
signanti tabulas, Charine, misi
Hyblaeis madidas thymis placentas.
defeci: miserere iam, Charine:
signa rarius, aut semel fac illud,
mentitur tua quod subinde tussis.
excussi loculosque sacculumque:
Croeso divitior licet fuissem,
Iro pauperior forem, Charine,
si conchem totiens meam comesses.

XLV

Dicis formonsam, dicis te, Bassa, puellam.
istud quae non est dicere, Bassa, solet.

39

Three times a month you change your will
And hopefully, with each codicil,
I send you cakes flavoured with honey
Of Hybla. Now that I've no money,
Have pity! Stop will-tinkering,
Charinus, or else do the thing
Long promised by that cough which mocks
Our expectations. My cash-box
Is drained, my purse has nothing in it.
Even if I became this minute
Richer than Croesus, I'd soon be
The beggar in the *Odyssey*:
At this rate, you'd exhaust my means
If all you got each time was beans.

45

Bassa, you tell us that you're young
And beautiful. Is it the truth?
That old refrain is often sung
By those who've lost both looks and youth.

XLVI

BASIA dum nolo nisi quae luctantia carpsi
et placet ira mihi plus tua quam facies,
ut te saepe rogem, caedo, Diadumene, saepe:
consequor hoc, ut me nec timeas nec ames.

LVI

CUI tradas, Lupe, filium magistro
quaeris sollicitus diu rogasque.
Omnes grammaticosque rhetorasque
devites moneo: nihil sit illi
cum libris Ciceronis aut Maronis,
famae Tutilium suae relinquat;
si versus facit, abdices poetam.
artes discere vult pecuniosas?
fac discat citharoedus aut choraules;
si duri puer ingeni videtur,
praeconem facias vel architectum.

46

The only kisses I enjoy
Are those I take by violence, boy.
Your anger whets my appetite
More than your face, and so to excite
Desire I give you a good beating
From time to time: a self-defeating
Habit – what do I do it for?
You neither fear nor love me more.

56

For ages you've been agonizing, bothering me with the
    problem: to which schoolmaster should you entrust your
    son?
Right, then. The boy should shun
Anyone who teaches
Grammar or rhetoric; let him steer clear of Virgil, skip
    Cicero's speeches
And leave Tutilius to stew in his own fame.
If he writes poetry, for the sake of the family name
Disinherit him. If it's money he wants to earn,
He can easily learn
To twang the harp in the chorus, or toot
The accompanist's flute.
If he seems short on intellect,
Make him an auctioneer or an architect.

LXXIV

POMPEIOS iuvenes Asia atque Europa, sed ipsum
    terra tegit Libyes, si tamen ulla tegit.
quid mirum toto si spargitur orbe? Iacere
    uno non poterat tanta ruina loco.

LXXVI

PROFECIT poto Mithridates saepe veneno
    toxica ne possent saeva nocere sibi.
tu quoque cavisti cenando tam male semper
    ne posses umquam, Cinna, perire fame.

LXXVIII

SI tristi domicenio laboras,
Torani, potes esurire mecum.
non derunt tibi, si soles προπίνειν,
viles Cappadocae gravesque porri,
divisis cybium latebit ovis.
ponetur digitis tenendus ustis
nigra coliculus virens patella,
algentem modo qui reliquit hortum,
et pultem niveam premens botellus,
et pallens faba cum rubente lardo.

74

Asia and Europe each provide a grave
For Pompey's sons, and he himself lies under
Egypt, if grave he can be said to have.
Or is the world his tomb? There'd be no wonder
In that: one monument would be too small
To house so huge, so ruinous a fall.

76

By daily making himself sick
With minuscule drops of arsenic
King Mithridates once built up
Immunity to the poison-cup.
In the same way, your small, vile dinner
Saves you from death by hunger, Cinna.

78

Toranius, if the prospect of a cheerless, solitary dinner
Bores you, eat with me – and get thinner.
If you like appetite-whetters,
There'll be cheap Cappadocian lettuce,
Pungent leeks, and tunny-fish
Nestling in sliced eggs. Next, a black earthenware dish
(Watch out – a finger-scorcher!) of broccoli just taken
From its cool bed, pale beans with pink bacon,
And a sausage sitting in the centre
Of a snow-white pudding of polenta.

Mensae munera si voles secundae,
marcentes tibi porrigentur uvae
et nomen pira quae ferunt Syrorum,
et quas docta Neapolis creavit,
lento castaneae vapore tostae:
vinum tu facies bonum bibendo.
Post haec omnia forte si movebit
Bacchus quam solet esuritionem,
succurrent tibi nobiles olivae,
Piceni modo quas tulere rami,
et fervens cicer et tepens lupinus.
Parva est cenula, — quis potest negare? —
sed finges nihil audiesve fictum
et voltu placidus tuo recumbes;
nec crassum dominus leget volumen,
nec de Gadibus inprobis puellae
vibrabunt sine fine prurientes
lascivos docili tremore lumbos;
sed quod nec grave sit nec infacetum,
parvi tibia Condyli sonabit.
Haec est cenula. Claudiam sequeris.
Quam nobis cupis esse tu priorem?

LXXXI

Semper pauper eris, si pauper es, Aemiliane.
dantur opes nullis nunc nisi divitibus.

If you want to try a dessert, I can offer you raisins (my
  own),
Pears (from Syria), and hot chestnuts (grown
In Naples, city of learning)
Roasted in a slow-burning
Fire. As for the wine, by drinking it you'll commend it.
When this great feast has ended,
If, as he well might,
Bacchus stirs up a second appetite,
You'll be reinforced by choice Picenian olives fresh from
  the trees,
Warm lupins and hot chick-peas.
Let's face it,
It's a poor sort of dinner; yet, if you deign to grace it,
You'll neither say nor hear
One word that's not sincere,
You can lounge at ease in your place,
Wearing your own face,
You won't have to listen while your host reads aloud from
  some thick book
Or be forced to look
At girls from that sink, Cadiz, prancing
Through the interminable writhings of professional belly-
  dancing.
Instead, Condylus, my little slave,
Will pipe to us – something not too rustic, nor yet too
  grave.
Well, that's the 'banquet'. I shall invite
Claudia to sit on my left. Who would you like on my right?

81

If you're poor now, my friend, then you'll stay poor.
These days only the rich get given more.

LIBER VI

XVII

CINNAM, Cinname, te iubes vocari.
non est hic, rogo, Cinna, barbarismus?
tu si Furius ante dictus esses,
Fur ista ratione dicereris.

XX

MUTUA te centum sestertia, Phoebe, rogavi,
   cum mihi dixisses 'Exigis ergo nihil?'
inquiris, dubitas, cunctaris meque diebus
   teque decem crucias: iam rogo, Phoebe, nega.

XLV

LUSISTIS, satis est: lascivi nubite cunni:
   permissa est vobis non nisi casta Venus.
Haec est casta Venus? nubit Laetoria Lygdo:
   turpior uxor erit quam modo moecha fuit.

BOOK SIX

17

'Address me,' you insist, 'as Long,'
Longbottom. The contraction's wrong.
Surely you wouldn't make the same
Mistake if Cockburn were your name?

20

'Why don't you ever ask a favour?'
'Then lend me a hundred,' I replied.
And now you stall and hedge and waver;
For ten whole days you've crucified
Our nerves – until I'm on my knees
Begging you, 'Phoebus, say no, please!'

45

Promiscuous girls, you've had your fun:
Now marry and 'cleave unto one'
   Lawfully. What a hope!
Laetoria, who's about to wed
Lygdus, will find the double bed
   Offers her twice the scope.

XLVI

VAPULAT adsidue veneti quadriga flagello
nec currit: magnam rem, Catiane, facit.

XLVIII

QUOD tam grande sophos clamat tibi turba togata,
non tu, Pomponi, cena diserta tua est.

LI

QUOD convivaris sine me tam saepe, Luperce,
   inveni noceam qua ratione tibi.
irascor: licet usque voces mittasque rogesque —
   'Quid facies?' inquis. Quid faciam? veniam.

46

The four-horse chariot of the Blues,
When Catianus plies the whip,
Drops back – to win the bribe and lose
The race. Consummate jockeyship!

48

Pomponius, when loud applause
Salutes you from your client-guests,
Don't fool yourself: good food's the cause
And not your after-dinner jests.

51

Because you're always giving splendid
Dinners and never ask me, I've
Planned my revenge. I'm so offended
By now that if you beg me, 'Please
Come to my house' on bended knees
I'll . . . what will I do to you? Arrive!

LII

Hoc iacet in tumulo raptus puerilibus annis
    Pantagathus, domini cura dolorque sui,
vix tangente vagos ferro resecare capillos
    doctus et hirsutas excoluisse genas.
sis licet, ut debes, tellus, placata levisque,
    artificis levior non potes esse manu.

LX

Laudat, amat, cantat nostros mea Roma libellos,
    meque sinus omnes, me manus omnis habet.
Ecce rubet quidam, pallet, stupet, oscitat, odit.
    hoc volo: nunc nobis carmina nostra placent.

LXIII

Scis te captari, scis hunc qui captat, avarum,
    et scis qui captat quid, Mariane, velit.
tu tamen hunc tabulis heredem, stulte, supremis
    scribis et esse tuo vis, furiose, loco.
'Munera magna tamen misit.' Sed misit in hamo;
    et piscatorem piscis amare potest?
hicine deflebit vero tua fata dolore?
    si cupis, ut ploret, des, Mariane, nihil.

52

His master's grief now, once his joy,
Here lies Pantagathus, a boy
So dexterous one could never feel
The touch when his tonsorial steel
Trimmed the unruly hairs or sheared
The stubble of a stubborn beard.
Earth, treat him, as is only right,
As gently as his hand was light.

60

All Rome is mad about my book:
It's praised, they hum the lines, shops stock it,
It peeps from every hand and pocket.
There's a man reading it! Just look –
He blushes, turns pale, reels, yawns, curses.
That's what I'm after. Bravo, verses!

63

You know you're being got at, you're aware
He's nothing but a fortune-hunting crook,
And yet, poor fool, you've named him as your heir
To step into your shoes. 'Ah, but he sent
Me presents that were quite magnificent.'
That was mere bait: didn't you spot the hook?
Can a fish love an angler? Do you believe
That he'll feel sorrow when you die? Just leave
Him nothing – then he'll genuinely grieve.

LXVI

Famae non nimium bonae puellam,
quales in media sedent Subura,
vendebat modo praeco Gellianus.
parvo cum pretio diu liceret,
dum puram cupit adprobare cunctis,
adtraxit prope se manu negantem
et bis terque quaterque basiavit.
Quid profecerit osculo requiris?
Sescentos modo qui dabat negavit.

LXXXII

Quidam me modo, Rufe, diligenter
inspectum, velut emptor aut lanista,
cum vultu digitoque subnotasset,
'Tune es, tune' ait 'ille Martialis,
cuius nequitias iocosque novit
aurem qui modo non habet Batavam?'
Subrisi modice, levique nutu
me quem dixerat esse non negavi.
'Cur ergo' inquis 'habes malas lacernas?'
Respondi: 'quia sum malus poeta.'
Hoc ne saepius accidat poetae,
mittas, Rufe, mihi bonas lacernas.

66

Last week, the auctioneer was trying to sell
A girl whose reputation one could smell
From here to her street corner in the slums.
After some time, when only paltry sums
Were being offered, wishing to assure
The crowd that she was absolutely pure,
He pulled the unwilling 'lot' across and smacked
Three or four kisses on her. Did this act
Make any difference to the price? It did.
The highest offerer withdrew his bid.

82

The other day, Rufus, somebody gave
Me the once-over, as though I were a slave
Or a gladiator open to inspection
At a sale. A thumb was jerked in my direction
Together with a surreptitious glance,
Then up he came: 'Are you by any chance
Martial, whose wicked epigrams are famous,
Whom everyone but a deaf Dutch ignoramus
Has heard of?' With a slight nod of the head
And a modest smile I bowed. 'Then why,' he said,
'Do you walk around wearing that terrible cloak?'
'Because I'm a terrible poet.' Terrible joke!
Rufus, to save me making it again,
Send me a cloak that keeps out the rain.

LIBER VII

III

Cur non mitto meos tibi, Pontiliane, libellos?
Ne mihi tu mittas, Pontiliane, tuos.

XI

Cogis me calamo manuque nostra
emendare meos, Pudens, libellos.
o quam me nimium probas amasque
qui vis archetypas habere nugas!

XVI

Aera domi non sunt, superest hoc, Regule, solum
ut tua vendamus munera: numquid emis?

BOOK SEVEN

3

Why have I never sent
My works to you, old hack?
For fear the compliment
Comes punishingly back.

11

Why do you press me to emend
My trifles with my own hand? Friend,
You're a flatterer. You know quite well
You'll keep the manuscript to sell.

16

At home I've empty coffers.
Only one thing can save me:
To sell the gifts you gave me.
Regulus, any offers?

XXXIX

Discursus varios vagumque mane
et fastus et have potentiorum
cum perferre patique iam negaret,
coepit fingere Caelius podagram.
quam dum volt nimis adprobare veram
et sanas linit obligatque plantas
inceditque gradu laborioso,
– quantum cura potest et ars doloris! –
desît fingere Caelius podagram.

XLIII

Primum est ut praestes, si quid te, Cinna, rogabo;
  illud deinde sequens ut cito, Cinna, neges.
diligo praestantem; non odi, Cinna, negantem:
  sed tu nec praestas nec cito, Cinna, negas.

39

Having had enough of early rising
And running around, of patronizing
'Good-mornings' or 'The great man's out',
Caelius decided to have gout.
He smeared and bandaged both his feet
And in his eagerness to complete
The imposture hobbled about wincing.
Such power has art, so self-convincing
Was Caelius, that at last his act
Translated fiction into fact.

43

Cinna, the best thing would be if you lent
Me anything I asked for. The next best
Would be for you to say no then and there.
I like good givers, and I don't resent
A straight refusal of a small request.
It's ditherers like you that I can't bear.

LIV

SEMPER mane mihi de me mera somnia narras,
    quae moveant animum sollicitentque meum.
iam prior ad faecem, sed et haec vindemia venit,
    exorat noctes dum mihi saga tuas;
consumpsi salsasque molas et turis acervos;
    decrevere greges, dum cadit agna frequens;
non porcus, non chortis aves, non ova supersunt.
    aut vigila aut dormi, Nasidiane, tibi.

LVIII

IAM sex aut septem nupsisti, Galla, cinaedis,
    dum coma te nimium pexaque barba iuvat.
deinde experta latus madidoque simillima loro
    inguina nec lassa stare coacta manu
deseris inbelles thalamos mollemque maritum,
    rursus et in similes decidis usque toros.
Quaere aliquem Curios semper Fabiosque loquentem,
    hirsutum et dura rusticitate trucem:
invenies: sed habet tristis quoque turba cinaedos:
    difficile est vero nubere, Galla, viro.

54

You tell me regularly every morning
Your dreams – dreams about me, of doom and warning,
Which worry me sick. Already, to appease
Heaven, I've poured to the expiatory lees
Both last and this year's wine; meanwhile I pay
The local witch to exorcize your grey
Forebodings. All my salt meal's used, I've finished
My stock of frankincense, my flock's diminished
By the huge quantity of lambs I've slain,
Not a pig, not a fowl, not even eggs remain.
Nasidianus, for our friendship's sake
Either dream of yourself or stay awake.

58

Galla, since you invariably fancy
Long hair and soft, combed beards, by now you've wed
Six or seven husbands, each of them a nancy.
Afterwards, when they've failed the test in bed
(Cocks like wet leather that won't get a stand on
However hard your hand pumps), you abandon
The weaponless field and the unmanly men –
And fall into the same old trap again.
Find some uncouth, rough-chinned philosopher
Who's always harping on the days that were!
You'll find one; but that grim 'old Roman' set
Is riddled with queers. Real men are hard to get.

LXI

Abstulerat totam temerarius institor urbem
    inque suo nullum limine limen erat.
iussisti tenuis, Germanice, crescere vicos,
    et modo quae fuerat semita, facta via est.
nulla catenatis pila est praecincta lagonis
    nec praetor medio cogitur ire luto,
stringitur in densa nec caeca novacula turba
    occupat aut totas nigra popina vias.
tonsor, copo, cocus, lanius sua limina servant.
    nunc Roma est, nuper magna taberna fuit.

61

The thrusting shopkeepers had long been poaching
Our city space, front premises encroaching
Everywhere. Then, Domitian, you commanded
That the cramped alleyways should be expanded,
And what were footpaths became real roads.
One doesn't see inn-posts, now, festooned with loads
Of chainéd flagons; the praetor walks the street
Without the indignity of muddy feet;
Razors aren't wildly waved in people's faces;
Bar-owners, butchers, barbers know their places,
And grimy restaurants can't spill out too far.
Now Rome is Rome, not just a huge bazaar.

LXXXVII

Si meus aurita gaudet lagalopece Flaccus,
 si fruitur tristi Canius Aethiope;
Publius exiguae si flagrat amore catellae,
 si Cronius similem cercopithecon amat;
delectat Marium si perniciosus ichneumon,
 pica salutatrix si tibi, Lause, placet;
si gelidum collo nectit Glaucilla draconem,
 luscinio tumulum si Telesilla dedit:
blanda Cupidinei cur non amet ora Labycae
 qui videt haec dominis monstra placere suis?

87

People have the oddest kinks.
My friend Flaccus fancies, ears and all, a lynx;
In Canius' opinion
You can't beat a coal-black Abyssinian;
Publius gets the itch
With a little terrier bitch;
Cronius is in love with a monkey that looks like him –
    almost human;
Marius cuddles a deadly ichneumon;
Lausus likes his talking magpie; Glaucilla, more reckless,
Coils her pet snake into a shivery necklace;
Telesilla,
When her nightingale died, erected a commemorative pillar.
Since it's every master to his own monstrous taste,
Why, sweet, Cupid-faced
Labycas, shouldn't you too be embraced?

LIBER VIII

XII

UXOREM quare locupletem ducere nolim
quaeritis? Uxori nubere nolo meae.
inferior matrona suo sit, Prisce, marito:
non aliter fiunt femina virque pares.

XXIII

ESSE tibi videor saevus nimiumque gulosus,
qui propter cenam, Rustice, caedo cocum.
si levis ista tibi flagrorum causa videtur,
ex qua vis causa vapulet ergo cocus?

XXVII

MUNERA qui tibi dat locupleti, Gaure, senique,
si sapis et sentis, hoc tibi ait 'Morere.'

XXIX

DISTICHA qui scribit, puto, vult brevitate placere.
quid prodest brevitas, dic mihi, si liber est?

BOOK EIGHT

12

Why have I no desire to marry riches?
Because, my friend, I want to wear the breeches.
Wives should obey their husbands; only then
Can women share equality with men.

23

Because my cook ruined the mutton
I thrashed him. You protested: 'Glutton!
Tyrant! The punishment should fit
The crime – you can't assault a man
For a spoilt dinner.' Yes, I can.
What worse crime can a cook commit?

27

If you were wise as well as rich and sickly,
You'd see that every gift means, 'Please die quickly.'

29

The epigrammatist's belief
Is that he pleases since he's terse.
But what's the use of being brief
At length – the length of a book of verse?

XXXV

Cum sitis similes paresque vita,
uxor pessima, pessimus maritus,
miror non bene convenire vobis.

XLI

'Tristis Athenagoras non misit munera nobis
quae medio brumae mittere mense solet.'
An sit Athenagoras tristis, Faustine, videbo:
me certe tristem fecit Athenagoras.

XLIII

Effert uxores Fabius, Chrestilla maritos,
funereamque toris quassat uterque facem.
victores committe, Venus: quos iste manebit
exitus una duos ut Libitina ferat.

35

Since you're alike and lead a similar life,
Horrible husband and ill-natured wife,
Why all the discord and domestic strife?

41

He says he's 'sorry' that he failed to send
My usual New Year's gift. A sorry friend!
How sorry, I'm not sure. At any rate
I know I too am in a sorry state.

43

Chrestilla digs her husbands' graves,
Fabius buries his wives. Each waves,
As bride or groom, the torch of doom
Over the marriage bed. Now pair
These finalists, Venus: let them share
Victory in a single tomb.

LXI

Livet Charinus, rumpitur, furit, plorat
et quaerit altos unde pendeat ramos:
non iam quod orbe cantor et legor toto,
nec umbilicis quod decorus et cedro
spargor per omnes Roma quas tenet gentes:
sed quod sub urbe rus habemus aestivum
vehimurque mulis non ut ante conductis.
Quid inprecabor, o Severe, liventi?
hoc opto: mulas habeat et suburbanum.

LXIX

Miraris veteres, Vacerra, solos
nec laudas nisi mortuos poetas.
ignoscas petimus, Vacerra: tanti
non est, ut placeam tibi, perire.

61

Charinus is ill with envy, bursting with it, weeping and
    raging and looking for high branches to commit suicide.
Why is he so mortified?
Not because the whole world's my admiring reader,
Nor because my book, smartly knobbed and dyed with oil
    of cedar,
Is passed from hand to hand among the nations that
    acknowledge Rome,
But simply because I've got a suburban summer home,
And mules to take me there, which I don't, as I used to
    have to, pay for.
What curse shall I pray for
To make him even iller?
His own mules, and a country villa.

69

    Rigidly classical, you save
    Your praise for poets in the grave.
    Forgive me, it's not worth my while
    Dying to earn your critical smile.

LXXI

Quattuor argenti libras mihi tempore brumae
    misisti ante annos, Postumiane, decem;
speranti plures – nam stare aut crescere debent
    munera – venerunt plusve minusve duae;
tertius et quartus multo inferiora tulerunt;
    libra fuit quinto Septiciana quidem;
besalem ad scutulam sexto pervenimus anno;
    post hunc in cotula rasa selibra data est;
octavus ligulam misit sextante minorem;
    nonus acu levius vix cocleare tulit.
quod mittat nobis decumus iam non habet annus:
    quattuor ad libras, Postumiane, redi.

LXXIX

Omnis aut vetulas habes amicas
aut turpis vetulisque foediores.
has ducis comites trahisque tecum
per convivia, porticus, theatra.
sic formonsa, Fabulla, sic puella es.

71

For New Year, Postumus, ten years ago,
You sent me four pounds of good silver-plate.
The next year, hoping for a rise in weight
(For gifts should either stay the same or grow),
I got two pounds. The third and fourth produced
Inferior presents, and the fifth year's weighed
Only a pound – Septicius' work, ill-made
Into the bargain. Next I was reduced
To an eight-ounce oblong salad-platter; soon
It was a miniature cup that tipped the scales
At even less. A tiny two-ounce spoon
Was the eighth year's surprise. The ninth, at length,
And grudgingly, disgorged a pick for snails
Lighter than a needle. Now, I note, the tenth
Has come and gone with nothing in its train.
I miss the old four pounds. Let's start again!

79

Her women friends are all old hags
Or, worse, hideous girls. She drags
Them with her everywhere she goes –
To parties, theatres, porticoes.
Clever Fabulla! Set among
Those foils you shine, even look young.

LIBER IX

IV

AUREOLIS futui cum possit Galla duobus
et plus quam futui, si totidem addideris:
aureolos a te cur accipit, Aeschyle, denos?
non fellat tanti Galla. Quid ergo? Tacet.

VI

DICERE de Libycis reduci tibi gentibus, Afer,
continuis volui quinque diebus Have:
'Non vacat' aut 'dormit' dictum est bis terque reverso.
Iam satis est: non vis, Afer, havere: vale.

IX

CENES, Canthare, cum foris libenter,
clamas et maledicis et minaris.
deponas animos truces monemus:
liber non potes et gulosus esse.

BOOK NINE

4

We all know Galla's services as a whore
Cost two gold bits; throw in a couple more
And you get the fancy extras too. Why, then,
Does your bill, Aeschylus, amount to ten?
She sucks off for far less than that. What is it
You pay her for? Silence after your visit.

6

On your return from Libya I tried
On five consecutive days to call and pay
My compliments. When I was turned away
Three times with 'He's asleep' or 'occupied',
I'd had enough. All right, if you're so shy,
Good-day, Afer, good riddance and good-bye.

9

Although you're glad to be asked out,
Whenever you go, you bitch and shout
And bluster. You must stop being rude:
You can't enjoy free speech *and* food.

XXXIII

Audieris in quo, Flacce, balneo plausum,
Maronis illic esse mentulam scito.

LX

Seu tu Paestanis genita es seu Tiburis arvis,
    seu rubuit tellus Tuscula flore tuo,
seu Praenestino te vilica legit in horto,
    seu modo Campani gloria ruris eras:
pulchrior ut nostro videare corona Sabino,
    de Nomentano te putet esse meo.

33

If from the baths you hear a round of applause,
Maron's giant prick is bound to be the cause.

60

Garland of roses, whether you come
From Tibur or from Tusculum,
Whether the earth you splashed with red
Was Paestum's or the flower-bed
Of some Praeneste farmer's wife
Who snipped you with her gardening-knife,
No matter in which countryside
You flew your flag before you died –
To lend my gift an added charm,
Let *him* believe you're from my farm.

LXVIII

Quid tibi nobiscum est, ludi scelerate magister,
  invisum pueris virginibusque caput?
nondum cristati rupere silentia galli:
  murmure iam saevo verberibusque tonas.
tam grave percussis incudibus aera resultant,
  causidicum medio cum faber aptat equo:
mitior in magno clamor furit amphitheatro,
  vincenti parmae cum sua turba favet.
vicini somnum – non tota nocte – rogamus:
  nam vigilare leve est, pervigilare grave est.
discipulos dimitte tuos. Vis, garrule, quantum
  accipis ut clames, accipere ut taceas?

68

Abominable schoolmaster, bogyman of little girls and
  boys,
We can do without you and your noise.
Before the crested cocks have shattered the night's silence
You're snarling, thundering, handing out corporal violence.
An anvil being banged to make a lawyer a bronze
  equestrian statue
Can't, for sheer din, match you,
Nor even the frenzied acclamation
Of the fans in the amphitheatre applauding their victorious
  Thracian.
We neighbours don't expect our nights to be unbroken:
It's a small nuisance to be occasionally woken,
But to lie sleepless is a disaster.
Send your pupils home, loud-mouthed schoolmaster.
Are you willing to take
As much to shut up as you earn for the row you make?

LXX

DIXERAT 'o mores! o tempora!' Tullius olim,
    sacrilegum strueret cum Catilina nefas,
cum gener atque socer diris concurreret armis
    maestaque civili caede maderet humus.
cur nunc 'o mores!' cur nunc 'o tempora!' dicis?
    quod tibi non placeat, Caeciliane, quid est?
nulla ducum feritas, nulla est insania ferri;
    pace frui certa laetitiaque licet.
Non nostri faciunt tibi quod tua tempora sordent,
    sed faciunt mores, Caeciliane, tui.

70

'Bad times! Bad morals!' good old Cicero
Exclaimed over a hundred years ago
When Catiline was plotting wicked war
Against the State, and father and son-in-law
Clashed, and the blood of our self-wounded nation
Drenched the poor earth. Why trot the trite quotation
Out now, Caecilianus? Why complain?
What's wrong? Our government is mild, the sane
Sword's in its sheath, and we're assured a lease
Of unobstructed happiness and peace.
If you think times are 'bad', by all means moan,
But don't accuse *our* morals – blame your own.

LXXXI

LECTOR et auditor nostros probat, Aule, libellos,
  sed quidam exactos esse poeta negat.
non nimium curo: nam cenae fercula nostrae
  malim convivis quam placuisse cocis.

LXXXV

LANGUIDIOR noster si quando est Paulus, Atili,
  non se, convivas abstinet ille suos.
Tu languore quidem subito fictoque laboras,
  sed mea porrexit sportula, Paule, pedes.

LXXXVIII

CUM me captares, mittebas munera nobis:
  postquam cepisti, das mihi, Rufe, nihil.
ut captum teneas, capto quoque munera mitte,
  de cavea fugiat ne male pastus aper.

81

Readers and listeners like my books,
Yet a certain poet calls them crude.
What do I care? I serve up food
To please my guests, not fellow cooks.

85

When Paulus has 'a sudden chill'
His guests lose more weight than their host.
He merely plays at being ill,
But our lost meal gives up the ghost.

88

When you were chasing my good will
You sent me gifts. You caught me. Then
The gifts stopped. You should send them still.
The ill-fed boar breaks from his pen.

LIBER X

VIII

Nubere Paula cupit nobis, ego ducere Paulam
nolo: anus est. Vellem, si magis esset anus.

XV

Cedere de nostris nulli te dicis amicis.
    sed, sit ut hoc verum, quid, rogo, Crispe, facis?
mutua cum peterem sestertia quinque, negasti,
    non caperet nummos cum gravis arca tuos.
quando fabae nobis modium farrisve dedisti,
    cum tua Niliacus rura colonus aret?
quando brevis gelidae missa est toga tempore brumae?
    argenti venit quando selibra mihi?
Nil aliud video quo te credamus amicum
    quam quod me coram pedere, Crispe, soles.

BOOK TEN

8

She longs for me to 'have and hold' her
In marriage. I've no mind to.
She's old. If she were even older,
I might be half inclined to.

15

Crispus, you're always saying you're the friend
Who loves me best. But your behaviour offers
No evidence for it. When I asked, 'Please lend
Five thousand,' you refused me though your coffers
Are crammed to bursting. And though fellaheen
Sweat on your profitable Nile estate
Have I had one ear of spelt from you, one bean?
Have you ever given me in the chilly season
A short-cut toga? Or sent silver-plate,
Even half a pound of it? I see no reason
Why I should count you as a friend – apart
From the informality with which you fart.

XVI

DOTATAE uxori cor harundine fixit acuta,
sed dum ludit Aper: ludere novit Aper.

XIX

NEC vocat ad cenam Marius, nec munera mittit,
nec spondet, nec volt credere, sed nec habet.
turba tamen non dest sterilem quae curet amicum.
Eheu! quam fatuae sunt tibi, Roma, togae!

XLIII

SEPTIMA iam, Phileros, tibi conditur uxor in agro.
Plus nulli, Phileros, quam tibi reddit ager.

16

Aper the archer's rich wife, struck
Through the heart by his own shaft, was killed.
All sports consist of skill and luck:
She was unlucky, he is skilled.

19

Marius doesn't entertain, or send
Presents, or stand as surety, or lend –
He hasn't got the money for it. Yet
A mob still courts this unrewarding 'friend'.
Clients of Rome, how stupid can you get!

43

Seven wives you've had – all dead
And buried in one field.
Of whom can it be said
His land gives richer yield?

XLVII

VITAM quae faciant beatiorem,
iucundissime Martialis, haec sunt:
res non parta labore sed relicta;
non ingratus ager, focus perennis;
lis numquam, toga rara, mens quieta;
vires ingenuae, salubre corpus;
prudens simplicitas, pares amici;
convictus facilis, sine arte mensa;
nox non ebria sed soluta curis;
non tristis torus et tamen pudicus;
somnus qui faciat breves tenebras:
quod sis esse velis nihilque malis;
summum nec metuas diem nec optes.

LIV

MENSAS, Ole, bonas ponis, sed ponis opertas.
Ridiculum est: possum sic ego habere bonas.

47

Of what does the happy life consist,
My dear friend, Julius? Here's a list:
Inherited wealth, no need to earn,
Fires that continually burn,
And fields that give a fair return,
No lawsuits, formal togas worn
Seldom, a calm mind, the freeborn
Gentleman's health and good physique,
Tact with the readiness to speak
Openly, friends of your own mind,
Guests of an easy-going kind,
Plain food, a table simply set,
Nights sober but wine-freed from fret,
A wife who's true to you and yet
No prude in bed, and sleep so sound
It makes the dawn come quickly round.
Be pleased with what you are, keep hope
Within that self-appointed scope;
Neither uneasily apprehend
Nor morbidly desire the end.

54

Your tables may, for all I know,
Be priceless; but that doesn't show
Under a cloth. Fool! Anyone's able
To own a covered 'antique' table.

LV

Arrectum quotiens Marulla penem
pensavit digitis diuque mensa est,
libras, scripula sextulasque dicit;
idem post opus et suas palaestras
loro cum similis iacet remisso,
quanto sit levior Marulla dicit.
Non ergo est manus ista, sed statera.

LIX

Consumpta est uno si lemmate pagina, transis,
    et breviora tibi, non meliora placent.
dives et ex omni posita est instructa macello
    cena tibi, sed te mattea sola iuvat.
Non opus est nobis nimium lectore guloso;
    hunc volo, non fiat qui sine pane satur.

55

Marulla's hobby is to measure
Erections. These she weighs at leisure
By hand and afterwards announces
Her estimate in pounds and ounces.
Once it's performed its exercise
And done its job and your cock lies
Rag-limp, again she'll calculate,
Manually, the loss in weight.
Hand? It's a grocer's balance-plate!

59

If an epigram takes up a page, you skip it:
Art counts for nothing, you prefer the snippet.
The markets have been ransacked for you, reader,
Rich fare – and you want canapés instead!
I'm not concerned with the fastidious feeder:
Give me the man who likes his basic bread.

LXI

Hic festinata requiescit Erotion umbra,
  crimine quam fati sexta peremit hiems.
quisquis eris nostri post me regnator agelli,
  manibus exiguis annua iusta dato:
sic lare perpetuo, sic turba sospite solus
  flebilis in terra sit lapis iste tua.

LXXIV

Iam parce lasso, Roma, gratulatori,
lasso clienti. Quamdiu salutator
anteambulones et togatulos inter
centum merebor plumbeos die toto,
cum Scorpus una quindecim graves hora
ferventis auri victor auferat saccos?
Non ego meorum praemium libellorum
– quid enim merentur? – Apulos velim campos;
non Hybla, non me spicifer capit Nilus,
nec quae paludes delicata Pomptinas
ex arce clivi spectat uva Setini.
Quid concupiscam quaeris ergo? Dormire.

61

Here, six years old, by Destiny's crime
Made a ghost before her time,
Erotion lies. Whoever you be,
Next lord of my small property,
See that the dues of death are paid
Annually to her slender shade:
So may your hearth burn bright and strong,
Your household thrive, yourself live long,
And this small stone, throughout the years,
Remain your only cause for tears.

74

Have mercy on me, Rome – a hired
Flatterer desperately tired
Of flattery! How long, how long,
Among the milling, toga'ed throng
Of parasites must I, for a whole
Day's work, bring back the worthless dole,
When Scorpus in his chariot
Gets fifteen sacks of gold, mint-hot,
In an hour? My books won't make me money:
I've never hoped for Hybla's honey,
Corn by the Nile, Apulian sheep
Or fine grapes that command the sweep
Of the Pontine marsh from Setia's crest.
Then what do I crave? One good night's rest.

LXXX

PLORAT Eros, quotiens maculosae pocula murrae
　inspicit aut pueros nobiliusve citrum,
et gemitus imo ducit de pectore quod non
　tota miser coëmat Saepta feratque domum.
Quam multi faciunt quod Eros sed lumine sicco!
　pars maior lacrimas ridet et intus habet.

LXXXV

IAM senior Ladon Tiberinae nauta carinae
　proxima dilectis rura paravit aquis.
quae cum saepe vagus premeret torrentibus undis
　Thybris et hiberno rumperet arva lacu,
emeritam puppim, ripa quae stabat in alta,
　inplevit saxis obposuitque vadis.
sic nimias avertit aquas. Quis credere posset?
　auxilium domino mersa carina tulit.

80

When Eros goes into a shop
And sees fine slaves, a table-top
Of citrus wood, a Murrine cup,
He weeps, he heaves his whole heart up
Because he can't, poor man, take home
The entire street! Thousands in Rome
Suffer the same pangs – but dry-eyed:
They mock his tears; *theirs* scald inside.

85

Ladon, the boatman, in retirement bought a
Plot by his dear old Tiber. When it spilled
Into his fields one winter and flood-water
Kept ruining them, what did he do? He filled
His superannuated boat with rocks
To form a barrier high up on the bank,
And staved off inundation. Paradox:
A skipper saved because his vessel sank!

XC

Quid vellis vetulum, Ligeia, cunnum?
quid busti cineres tui lacessis?
tales munditiae decent puellas –
nam tu iam nec anus potes videri –;
istud, crede mihi, Ligeia, belle
non mater facit Hectoris, sed uxor.
Erras si tibi cunnus hic videtur,
ad quem mentula pertinere desît.
quare si pudor est, Ligeia, noli
barbam vellere mortuo leoni.

XCIV

Non mea Massylus servat pomaria serpens,
  regius Alcinoi nec mihi servit ager,
sed Nomentana securus germinat hortus
  arbore, nec furem plumbea mala timent.
Haec igitur media quae sunt modo nata Subura
  mittimus autumni cerea poma mei.

90

Why poke the ash of a dead fire?
Why pluck the hairs from your grey fanny?
That's a chic touch which men admire
In girls, not in a flagrant granny;
Something, believe me, which might suit
Andromache but looks far from cute
In Hecuba. Ligeia, you err
If you think sex could rear its head
To burrow in your mangy fur.
Remember what the wise man said:
'Don't pluck the lion's beard when he's dead.'

94

My orchard isn't the Hesperides,
There's no Massylian dragon at the gate,
Nor is it King Alcinous' estate;
It's in Nomentum, where the apple-trees,
Perfectly unmolested, bear a crop
So tasteless that no guard needs to be kept –
Thieves wouldn't bother. And so please accept
My harvest offering, fresh-picked – from a shop.

XCVII

Dum levis arsura struitur Libitina papyro,
  dum murram et casias flebilis uxor emit,
iam scrobe, iam lecto, iam pollinctore parato,
  heredem scripsit me Numa: convaluit.

97

Laid with papyrus to catch fire
And lightly heaped, the funeral pyre
Was all prepared, the wife was buying
Myrrh and cinnamon, and crying,
The grave, the bier, the corpse-perfumer
Were ready, when the dying Numa
Declared his previous will invalid,
Named me as heir – and promptly rallied.

LIBER XI

XVII

Non omnis nostri nocturna est pagina libri:
invenies et quod mane, Sabine, legas.

XVIII

Donasti, Lupe, rus sub urbe nobis;
sed rus est mihi maius in fenestra.
rus hoc dicere, rus potes vocare?
in quo ruta facit nemus Dianae,
argutae tegit ala quod cicadae,
quod formica die comedit uno,
clusae cui folium rosae corona est;
in quo non magis invenitur herba
quam Cosmi folium piperve crudum;
in quo nec cucumis iacere rectus
nec serpens habitare tota possit.
urucam male pascit hortus unam,
consumpto moritur culix salicto,
et talpa est mihi fossor atque arator.
non boletus hiare, non mariscae
ridere aut violae patere possunt.
finis mus populatur et colono

BOOK ELEVEN

17

Not all the epigrams I write
Belong to naughtiness and the night:
You'll find a few that can be read
Before midday, with a clear head.

18

Lupus, I'm deeply in your debt
For this suburban 'farm'; and yet
My window-box in Rome's as big.
Do you call this an 'estate'? A sprig
Of rue here seems Diana's wood;
The wing of one cicada could
Umbrella it; an ant devours
The property within twelve hours;
A rose-petal would wrap it round;
There's not a grass-blade to be found,
Not a leaf to crush to make perfume,
Not a pepper plant, not even room
For a cucumber to lie straight
Or a snake to stretch. The whole 'estate'
Unsatisfactorily supplies
A single caterpillar; flies
Die of starvation once they've fed
On the diminutive willow-bed;
A mole's my ploughman and ditch-digger;
Mushrooms won't venture to grow bigger,
Violets can't smile, figs daren't expand.
The dragon of my hinterland
Is a mouse, feared by the farmer more

tamquam sus Calydonius timetur,
et sublata volantis ungue Prognes
in nido seges est hirundinino;
et cum stet sine falce mentulaque,
non est dimidio locus Priapo.
vix implet cocleam peracta messis,
et mustum nuce condimus picata.
Errasti, Lupe, littera sed una:
nam quo tempore praedium dedisti,
mallem tu mihi prandium dedisses.

XIX

QUAERIS cur nolim te ducere, Galla? Diserta es.
saepe soloecismum mentula nostra facit.

XXIV

DUM te prosequor et domum reduco,
aurem dum tibi praesto garrienti,
et quidquid loqueris facisque laudo,
quot versus poterant, Labulle, nasci!
hoc damnum tibi non videtur esse,
si quod Roma legit, requirit hospes,
non deridet eques, tenet senator,
laudat causidicus, poeta carpit,

Than the great Calydonian boar;
The swallow's claw steals all my crop
To wall her nest; and though I lop
His sickle and priapic rod
There's no space for the garden god.
A snail-shell barely can contain
The harvest of my gathered grain
And, as for grapes, a pitch-sealed nut
Stores a year's vintage. Thank you . . . but
Your gift miscarried by one letter:
For 'rood' read 'food' – and I'd live better.

19

Why won't I marry you? You're a blue-stocking,
And my cock's educated something shocking.

24

Labullus, I court you,
I escort you, I support you
By lending an ear to your chatter,
And everything you say or do I flatter.
Meanwhile how many verses have died stillborn in my
    inspiration!
Doesn't it strike you as a grave loss to the nation
That, because of you, poems should perish
Which all Rome reads, foreigners ask for, knights think
    well of, senators cherish,
Barristers praise to the skies
And poets – criticize?

propter te perit – hoc, Labulle, verum est – ?
hoc quisquam ferat? ut tibi tuorum
sit maior numerus togatulorum,
librorum mihi sit minor meorum?
Triginta prope iam diebus una est
nobis pagina vix peracta. Sic fit
cum cenare domi poeta non vult.

XXIX

Languida cum vetula tractare virilia dextra
  coepisti, iugulor pollice, Phylli, tuo:
nam cum me murem, cum me tua lumina dicis,
  horis me refici vix puto posse decem.
Blanditias nescis: 'dabo' dic 'tibi milia centum
  et dabo Setini iugera culta soli;
accipe vina, domum, pueros, chrysendeta, mensas.'
  Nil opus est digitis: sic mihi, Phylli, frica.

It's intolerable. It's not right
That just so that you can have one more toga'd little
  parasite
The number of my books should be diminished.
It's almost a month now, and I've scarcely finished
A single page. Well, that's Rome
For a poet who hates dining at home.

29

Phyllis, when your old claws attempt to strum
My instrument, I'm half-throttled by your thumb,
And when you call me 'mouse' or 'precious lover'
It takes me over twelve hours to recover.
You've no idea how to make love. Say, 'Please
Accept a hundred thousand sesterces'
Or, 'Have some farmland – here's a large estate
In Setia' or, 'Take this antique plate,
My wines, slaves, tables, or my house in town.'
That's the right way to rub me – up, not down.

XXXV

Ignotos mihi cum voces trecentos,
quare non veniam vocatus ad te
miraris quererisque litigasque.
Solus ceno, Fabulle, non libenter.

XXXIX

Cunarum fueras motor, Charideme, mearum
et pueri custos adsiduusque comes.
iam mihi nigrescunt tonsa sudaria barba
et queritur labris puncta puella meis;
sed tibi non crevi: te noster vilicus horret,
te dispensator, te domus ipsa pavet.
ludere nec nobis nec tu permittis amare;
nil mihi vis et vis cuncta licere tibi.
corripis, observas, quereris, suspiria ducis,
et vix a ferulis temperat ira tua.
si Tyrios sumpsi cultus unxive capillos,
exclamas 'Numquam fecerat ista pater';
et numeras nostros adstricta fronte trientes,
tamquam de cella sit cadus ille tua.
Desine; non possum libertum ferre Catonem.
esse virum iam me dicet amica tibi.

35

Three hundred guests, not one of whom I know –
And you, as host, wonder that I won't go.
Don't quarrel with me, I'm not being rude:
I can't enjoy sociable solitude.

39

You rocked my cradle, Charidemus, gave
Me constant care and guidance while I grew;
Yet now, although the towel's black when I shave
And my girl scolds my prickly kiss, to you
I'm still a child. You bully my bailiff, cow
My steward, make the very building quake.
You ban fun, you bar girls, you won't allow
Me liberties – although you're pleased to take
Plenty yourself! You nag, spy, grumble, sigh,
Itching to use the old tutorial stick
Whenever you're irascible. 'Oh,' you cry,
'Your father never did that!' if I slick
My hair with scent or sport a purple cloak,
And when I drink you frown and count each cup
As though it came from your own cellar. The joke
Has gone too far. I can't, I won't put up
With an ex-slave aping Cato. I'm a man:
If you can't see that, ask my girl – *she* can.

LVI

QUOD nimium mortem, Chaeremon Stoice, laudas,
　　vis animum mirer suspiciamque tuum?
hanc tibi virtutem fracta facit urceus ansa,
　　et tristis nullo qui tepet igne focus,
et teges et cimex et nudi sponda grabati,
　　et brevis atque eadem nocte dieque toga.
O quam magnus homo es qui faece rubentis aceti
　　et stipula et nigro pane carere potes!
Leuconicis agedum tumeat tibi culcita lanis
　　constringatque tuos purpura pexa toros,
dormiat et tecum qui cum modo Caecuba miscet
　　convivas roseo torserat ore puer:
o quam tu cupies ter vivere Nestoris annos
　　et nihil ex ulla perdere luce voles!
Rebus in angustis facile est contemnere vitam:
　　fortiter ille facit qui miser esse potest.

56

Because you glorify death, old Stoic,
Don't expect me to admire you as heroic.
What does your high-mindedness amount to but a few
    broken-handled jugs,
A cheerless, fireless hearth, some moth-eaten rugs,
A bare bed-frame, a cut-down toga (worn day and night)
    and bugs?
What a spiritual achievement – to be able to do without
    straw for your bed,
Sour red wine and cheap black bread!
Come off it! Imagine yourself tucked up asleep
Under thick purple quilts, on pillows bulging with the wool
    of Leuconian sheep,
In the arms of a red-lipped boy who's just filled your guests'
    cups to the brim
And made them long for a taste of him.
Ah, be honest, then you'd pray
To live three times as long as Nestor, to savour every
    minute of every day.
It's easy to despise life when things go wrong:
The true hero endures much, and long.

LVII

MIRARIS docto quod carmina mitto Severo,
    ad cenam cum te, docte Severe, vocem?
Iuppiter ambrosia satur est et nectare vivit;
    nos tamen exta Iovi cruda merumque damus.
omnia cum tibi sint dono concessa deorum,
    si quod habes non vis, ergo quid accipies?

LXII

LESBIA se iurat gratis numquam esse fututam.
    Verum est. Cum futui vult, numerare solet.

LXVI

ET delator es et calumniator,
et fraudator es et negotiator,
et fellator es et lanista. Miror
quare non habeas, Vacerra, nummos.

57

Does it surprise you, my dear poet friend,
That when I ask you round to dine I send
Some lines of verse? Though Jupiter has his fill
Of nectar and ambrosia, we still
Offer him wine and entrails in a dish.
The gods have given you all a man could wish:
Since you can't want what you've already got,
To send you something begs the question, what?

62

Lesbia claims she's never laid
Without good money being paid.
That's true enough: when she's on fire
She'll always pay the hose's hire.

66

You're an informer and a tool of slander
And a notorious swindler and a pander
And a cock-sucker and a gangster and a . . .
I can't make out, Vacerra, why you're poor.

LXVII

NIL mihi das vivus; dicis post fata daturum.
Si non es stultus, scis, Maro, quid cupiam.

LXVIII

PARVA rogas magnos; sed non dant haec quoque magni.
Ut pudeat levius te, Matho, magna roga.

LXXI

HYSTERICAM vetulo se dixerat esse marito
et queritur futui Leda necesse sibi;
sed flens atque gemens tanti negat esse salutem
seque refert potius proposuisse mori.
vir rogat ut vivat virides nec deserat annos,
et fieri quod iam non facit ipse sinit.
protinus accedunt medici medicaeque recedunt,
tollunturque pedes. O medicina gravis!

67

You give me nothing now. 'Ah, yes,'
You say, 'but you're one of my heirs.'
Unless you're stupid, you can guess
How hopefully I say my prayers.

68

You ask great men small favours, yet
The little asked you never get.
It would be kinder to your pride
To beg more – and still be denied.

71

One day Leda announced to her aged husband, 'I'm
suffering from hysteria.
I'm sorry, but I'm told that nothing but intercourse will
make me feel cheerier.'
In the same tearful breath
She swore his honour mattered more than her health, she
preferred a martyr's death.
Her lord and master urged her to preserve her life and
beauty
And gave permission for the vicarious performance of his
duty.
At once the nurses retire, the doctors rush in,
Hoist and prise open her legs. Ah, sweet medicine!

LXXIII

VENTURUM iuras semper mihi, Lygde, roganti
  constituisque horam constituisque locum.
cum frustra iacui longa prurigine tentus,
  succurrit pro te saepe sinistra mihi.
Quid precer, o fallax, meritis et moribus istis?
  umbellam luscae, Lygde, feras dominae.

LXXVII

IN omnibus Vacerra quod conclavibus
consumit horas et die toto sedet,
cenaturit Vacerra, non cacaturit.

XCVI

MARCIA, non Rhenus, salit hic, Germane: quid opstas
  et puerum prohibes divitis imbre lacus?
barbare, non debet, summoto cive, ministro
  captivam victrix unda levare sitim.

73

Whenever I say, 'Please come,' you always swear
You will, and you yourself fix when and where.
I'm there all right, but usually, after I've lain
Interminably frustrated, stiff with strain,
My left hand helps me out – sad substitute.
Lygdus, what curse can I devise to suit
A stander-up like you? May you be made
To carry a one-eyed harridan's sunshade!

77

For hours, for a whole day, he'll sit
On every public lavatory seat.
It's not because he needs a shit:
He wants to be asked out to eat.

96

German, this is our aqueduct
And not the Rhine. Barbarian clot,
How dare you elbow and obstruct
A thirsty boy from drinking? What!
Jostle a Roman from his place!
This is the conqueror's fountain, not
A trough for your defeated race.

XCVIII

EFFUGERE non est, Flacce, basiatores.
instant, morantur, persecuntur, occurrunt
et hinc et illinc, usquequaque, quacumque.
non ulcus acre pusulaeve lucentes,
nec triste mentum sordidique lichenes,
nec labra pingui delibuta cerato,
nec congelati gutta proderit nasi.
et aestuantem basiant et algentem,
et nuptiale basium reservantem.
non te cucullis adseret caput tectum,
lectica nec te tuta pelle veloque,
nec vindicabit sella saepius clusa:
rimas per omnis basiator intrabit.
non consulatus ipse, non tribunatus
senive fasces nec superba clamosi
lictoris abiget virga basiatorem:
sedeas in alto tu licet tribunali
et e curuli iura gentibus reddas,
ascendet illa basiator atque illa.
febricitantem basiabit et flentem,
dabit oscitanti basium natantique,
dabit cacanti. Remedium mali solum est,
facias amicum basiare quem nolis.

98

There's no escaping the kissers, Flaccus.
They ambush us, attack us,
Waylay us,
Delay us
At all times of day, wherever you go or I go.
Ulcers, weeping sores, filthy scabs, impetigo,
Salve-smeared lips,
A nose with stalactitic drips,
An ice-cold cheek, a sweat-soaked face,
Even a mouth reserved for your bride's embrace
Won't save you. It's useless to resist:
You're doomed to be kissed.
Wrap your head in a hood, travel in a double-curtained
  litter or a sedan with a multiple barrier,
There'll still be a chink for an osculatory harrier.
Become consul, tribune, praetor with six booming, crowd-
  clearing lictors with rods and axes,
Sit on the curule chair, in the high tribunal, dealing justice
  to the nations – there's no prophylaxis:
Whether you're crying,
Half-dying,
Yawning, swimming or pissing,
Someone will clamber up and start kissing.
There's only one remedy. It's this:
Make friends with people you don't want to kiss.

XCIX

DE cathedra quotiens surgis – iam saepe notavi –
    pedicant miserae, Lesbia, te tunicae.
quas cum conata es dextra, conata sinistra
    vellere, cum lacrimis eximis et gemitu:
sic constringuntur magni Symplegade culi
    et nimias intrant Cyaneasque natis.
Emendare cupis vitium deforme? docebo:
    Lesbia, nec surgas censeo nec sedeas.

C

HABERE amicam nolo, Flacce, subtilem,
cuius lacertos anuli mei cingant,
quae clune nudo radat et genu pungat,
cui serra lumbis, cuspis eminet culo.
sed idem amicam nolo mille librarum.
Carnarius sum, pinguiarius non sum.

99

Whenever you rise from a chair, Lesbia, your wretched
    clothes jump,
Like buggers, right up your rump –
I've often observed the sight.
You try twitching them to the left or the right
And finally wrench them free with a tearful shriek,
So deep is the creek they've sailed up, so fierce the squeeze
Of those huge twin Symplegades.
Would you like to cure this unattractive defect? Do you
    want my advice? This is it:
Don't get up – and never sit.

100

Flaccus, the sort of girl I hate
Is the scrawny one, with arms so thin
My rings would fit them, hips that grate,
Spine like a saw, knee like a pin
And a coccyx like a javelin.
But all the same I don't go in
For sheer bulk. I appreciate
Good meat, not blubber, on my plate.

CII

NON est mentitus qui te mihi dixit habere
  formonsam carnem, Lydia, non faciem.
est ita, si taceas et si tam muta recumbas
  quam silet in cera vultus et in tabula.
sed quotiens loqueris, carnem quoque, Lydia, perdis
  et sua plus nulli quam tibi lingua nocet.
Audiat aedilis ne te videatque caveto:
  portentum est, quotiens coepit imago loqui.

CIII

TANTA tibi est animi probitas orisque, Safroni,
  ut mirer fieri te potuisse patrem.

CIV

UXOR, vade foras aut moribus utere nostris:
  non sum ego nec Curius nec Numa nec Tatius.
me iucunda iuvant tractae per pocula noctes:
  tu properas pota surgere tristis aqua.
tu tenebris gaudes: me ludere teste lucerna
  et iuvat admissa rumpere luce latus.
fascia te tunicaeque obscuraque pallia celant;
  at mihi nulla satis nuda puella iacet.
basia me capiunt blandas imitata columbas:
  tu mihi das aviae qualia mane soles.

102

Whoever said of you, 'She's all complexion
And no expression,' Lydia, scored a hit.
Sit like a waxwork or a studio peach
And keep your mouth shut, and you're exquisite.
But the first word ruins that perfection:
You're utterly disqualified by speech.
Don't let the aediles hear you. If they catch you,
They'll class you as a portent – talking statue!

103

Safronius, you look so meek and mild
I can't imagine how you got your child.

104

Either get out of the house or conform to my tastes, woman.
I'm no strait-laced old Roman.
I like prolonging the nights agreeably with wine: you, after
   one glass of water,
Rise and retire with an air of hauteur.
You prefer darkness: I enjoy love-making
With a witness – a lamp shining or the dawn breaking.
You wear bed-jackets, tunics, thick woollen stuff,
Whereas I think no woman on her back can ever be naked
   enough.
I love girls who kiss like doves and hang round my neck:
You give me the sort of peck
Due to your grandmother as a morning salute.

nec motu dignaris opus nec voce iuvare
   nec digitis, tamquam tura merumque pares:
masturbabantur Phrygii post ostia servi,
   Hectoreo quotiens sederat uxor equo,
et quamvis Ithaco stertente pudica solebat
   illic Penelope semper habere manum.
pedicare negas: dabat hoc Cornelia Graccho,
   Iulia Pompeio, Porcia, Brute, tibi;
dulcia Dardanio nondum miscente ministro
   pocula Iuno fuit pro Ganymede Iovi.
Si te delectat gravitas, Lucretia toto
   sis licet usque die, Laida nocte volo.

CVIII

Quamvis tam longo possis satur esse libello,
   lector, adhuc a me disticha pauca petis.
sed Lupus usuram puerique diaria poscunt.
   Lector, solve. Taces dissimulasque? Vale.

In bed, you're motionless, mute –
Not a wriggle,
Not a giggle –
As solemn as a priestess at a shrine
Proffering incense and pure wine.
Yet every time Andromache went for a ride
In Hector's room, the household slaves used to masturbate
   outside;
Even modest Penelope, when Ulysses snored,
Kept her hand on the sceptre of her lord.
You refuse to be buggered; but it's a known fact
That Gracchus', Pompey's and Brutus' wives were willing
   partners in the act,
And that before Ganymede mixed Jupiter his tasty bowl
Juno filled the dear boy's role.
If you want to be uptight – all right,
By all means play Lucretia by day. But I need a Laïs at
   night.

108

I should have thought you'd had your fill
By now – this book's too long – yet still
You clamour for couplets. You forget,
My slaves need rations, I'm in debt,
The interest's due. . . . Dear reader, pay
My creditors for me. Silent, eh?
The puzzled innocent? Good-day!

LIBER XII

XII

OMNIA promittis cum tota nocte bibisti;
mane nihil praestas. Pollio, mane bibe.

XIII

GENUS, Aucte, lucri divites habent iram:
odisse quam donare vilius constat.

XVIII

DUM tu forsitan inquietus erras
clamosa, Iuvenalis, in Subura
aut collem dominae teris Dianae;
dum per limina te potentiorum
sudatrix toga ventilat vagumque
maior Caelius et minor fatigant:
me multos repetita post Decembres
accepit mea rusticumque fecit
auro Bilbilis et superba ferro.
Hic pigri colimus labore dulci
Boterdum Plateamque – Celtiberis
haec sunt nomina crassiora terris – :
ingenti fruor inproboque somno
quem nec tertia saepe rumpit hora,
et totum mihi nunc repono quidquid
ter denos vigilaveram per annos.

BOOK TWELVE

12

Whenever you drink all night you make
Huge promises, which next day you break.
Booze in the morning – for *my* sake.

13

The rich know anger helps the cost of living:
Hating's more economical than giving.

18

While you're, no doubt, anxiously threading
Rome's noisiest, nastiest streets, or treading
Sovereign Diana's Aventine,
Or sweating in a clients' line
(Soaked toga serving as a fan)
In the ante-room of some great man,
Or slogging up or stumbling down
Both Caelian hills, my own home town
Bilbilis, proud of iron and gold,
Has welcomed back into the fold
Me revenant after many a year
And made me truly rural. Here,
A son of undemanding toil,
I gently farm Boterdum's soil
(These uncouth Spanish names!) and sleep
Past nine, grossly, shamefully deep,
Thus catching up on the arrears
Of thirty-odd insomniac years.

Ignota est toga, sed datur petenti
rupta proxima vestis a cathedra.
surgentem focus excipit superba
vicini strue cultus iliceti,
multa vilica quem coronat olla.
venator sequitur, sed ille quem tu
secreta cupias habere silva;
dispensat pueris rogatque longos
levis ponere vilicus capillos.
Sic me vivere, sic iuvat perire.

XXVIII

Hermogenes tantus mapparum, Castrice, fur est
  quantus nummorum vix, puto, Massa fuit;
tu licet observes dextram teneasque sinistram,
  inveniet mappam qua ratione trahat:
cervinus gelidum sorbet sic halitus anguem,
  casuras alte sic rapit Iris aquas.
nuper cum Myrino peteretur missio laeso,
  subduxit mappas quattuor Hermogenes;
cretatam praetor cum vellet mittere mappam,
  praetori mappam surpuit Hermogenes.
attulerat mappam nemo dum furta timentur:
  mantele a mensa surpuit Hermogenes.

The toga's unknown: if I shout
For clothes I'm given the nearest clout
From a broken chair. Once out of bed,
A fire greets me, royally fed
With oak-logs from our local copse,
Which my young bailiff's wife then tops
With bubbling pots. Enter a boy,
My 'huntsman' (one you'd love to enjoy
In a quiet wood, Juvenal). On his heels
The smooth-cheeked bailiff comes and deals
The slaves their rations. Will I let
Him cut the youngsters' hair and set
Them a man's work? he wants to know.
This is the life for me; and so,
Easy I live, content I'll go.

28

Hermogenes steals napkins on the same scale as Massa
    embezzled money in Spain.
A master of legerdemain!
Keep your eyes on his right hand, pinion his left,
And he'll still bring off a theft
As marvellously as a stag, by inhaling, swallows a clammy
    snake
Or the rainbow smuggles the next shower up from the lake.
Last week, when the praetor was about to start a chariot-
    race with his white flag, before he'd twitched it
Hermogenes had snitched it;
And when Myrino, wounded, appealed for mercy and the
    crowd waved a unanimous handkerchief,

hoc quoque si derit, medios discingere lectos
  mensarumque pedes non timet Hermogenes.
quamvis non modico caleant spectacula sole,
  vela reducuntur cum venit Hermogenes.
festinant trepidi substringere carbasa nautae,
  ad portum quotiens paruit Hermogenes.
linigeri fugiunt calvi sistrataque turba,
  inter adorantes cum stetit Hermogenes.
ad cenam Hermogenes mappam non attulit umquam,
  a cena semper rettulit Hermogenes.

xxx

Siccus, sobrius est Aper; quid ad me?
servum sic ego laudo, non amicum.

Four were filched by the same thief.
When apprehensive guests arrive without their own napery,
He takes the table-cloth or, failing that, pelmets, couch-
    covers, dust-sheets, any old drapery.
Even when the arena's so hot that spectators swelter,
If Hermogenes turns up they hurriedly roll back the sun-
    shelter.
When he shows his face at the port,
The nervous sailors haul their canvas short.
When he mingles with the worshippers of Isis,
There's a panic crisis
Among the bald, linen-clad priests and the drum-beating
    devotees.
We all know Hermogenes
Never brings a napkin when he's asked to dine,
But he always takes one home – yours or mine.

30

Aper's teetotal. So what? I commend
Sobriety in a butler, not a friend.

XXXI

Hoc nemus, hi fontes, haec textilis umbra supini
    palmitis, hoc riguae ductile flumen aquae,
prataque nec bifero cessura rosaria Paesto,
    quodque viret Iani mense nec alget holus,
quaeque natat clusis anguilla domestica lymphis,
    quaeque gerit similes candida turris aves,
munera sunt dominae: post septima lustra reverso
    has Marcella domos parvaque regna dedit.
Si mihi Nausicaa patrios concederet hortos,
    Alcinoo possem dicere 'Malo meos.'

31

Wood, fields and streams, this latticed shade
Of vine, my conduits and cascade,
My roses which can challenge those
That super-fertile Paestum grows,
My vegetables, frost-immune
And green in January as June,
My private tank where tame eels swim,
My dovecot just as white and trim
As its own inmates – everything
In the small realm of which I'm king
Was given me by my patroness
And friend, Marcella (whom heaven bless),
When I returned to Spain and home
After thirty-five years in Rome.
If Nausicaa's father were
To make me the inheritor
Of his famous gardens and his throne,
I could say, 'I prefer my own.'

XXXIV

TRIGINTA mihi quattuorque messes
tecum, si memini, fuere, Iuli.
quarum dulcia mixta sunt amaris
sed iucunda tamen fuere plura;
et si calculus omnis huc et illuc
diversus bicolorque digeratur,
vincet candida turba nigriorem.
Si vitare velis acerba quaedam
et tristis animi cavere morsus,
nulli te facias nimis sodalem:
gaudebis minus et minus dolebis.

XL

MENTIRIS, credo: recitas mala carmina, laudo:
   cantas, canto: bibis, Pontiliane, bibo:
pedis, dissimulo: gemma vis ludere, vincor:
   res una est sine me quam facis, et taceo.
nil tamen omnino praestas mihi. 'Mortuus,' inquis,
   'accipiam bene te.' Nil volo: sed morere.

34

If memory serves, we've shared together
Thirty-four years, Julius. Weather
Both fair and foul as friends we've had,
Yet good times have outnumbered bad.
Indeed, if we were to divide
The days by pebbles – on one side
Black, on the other white – the higher
Heap would be bright. If you desire
To avoid the acid taste of life
And to be proof against the knife
That stabs the heart, follow my plan:
Don't come too close to any man.
That way your pleasure may be less,
So also will your bitterness.

40

You tell lies – I lend a credulous ear;
You recite bad poems – I raise a loyal cheer;
You sing – I join in; you drink – I drink with you; you fart
  – I pretend not to hear;
You want to play draughts – I gracefully yield.
There's only one thing you do without my complicity, and
  on that subject my lips remain sealed.
For all this I get absolutely nil.
'Ah, but in my will
I'll remember you,' you say.
I want nothing. Still, roll on, that day.

XLVI

DIFFICILIS facilis, iucundus acerbus es idem:
nec tecum possum vivere nec sine te.

LVI

AEGROTAS uno decies aut saepius anno,
    nec tibi sed nobis hoc, Polycharme, nocet:
nam quotiens surgis, soteria poscis amicos.
    Sit pudor: aegrota iam, Polycharme, semel.

LXI

VERSUS et breve vividumque carmen
in te ne faciam times, Ligurra,
et dignus cupis hoc metu videri.
sed frustra metuis cupisque frustra.
In tauros Libyci ruunt leones,
non sunt papilionibus molesti.
Quaeras censeo, si legi laboras,
nigri fornicis ebrium poetam,
qui carbone rudi putrique creta
scribit carmina quae legunt cacantes.
Frons haec stigmate non meo notanda est.

46

Amiable but unco-operative,
   Sweet-natured but a grouse —
Though I can't live without you, I can live
   Without you in the house.

56

Ten times a year or more you catch a chill.
The suffering's ours, though, for you levy presents
All round in honour of each convalescence.
Think of your friends. Be seriously ill!

61

You say you're scared I'm going to aim
A lampoon at you, something brief
And lurid, and half proudly claim
You're a marked man. Wishful belief!
Misapprehended apprehension!
African lions pay attention
To bulls, they don't hunt butterflies.
Ligurra, since you've such a hunger
For public notice, I advise
Hiring some sozzled ballad-monger
In a smoke-blackened dive who scrawls
Graffiti over lavatory walls
With stubs of mouldy chalk or coal.
I wouldn't touch you with a pole.

LXVIII

Matutine cliens, urbis mihi causa relictae,
    atria, si sapias, ambitiosa colas.
non sum ego causidicus nec amaris litibus aptus
    sed piger et senior Pieridumque comes;
otia me somnusque iuvant, quae magna negavit
    Roma mihi: redeo, si vigilatur et hic.

LXXIII

Heredem tibi me, Catulle, dicis.
non credam, nisi legero, Catulle.

68

Poor morning client (you remind me
Of all I loathed and left behind me
In Rome), if you had any nous,
Instead of calling on my house
You'd haunt the mansions of the great.
I'm not some wealthy advocate
Blessed with a sharp, litigious tongue,
I'm just a lazy, far from young
Friend of the Muses who likes ease
And sleep. Great Rome denied me these:
If I can't find them even in Spain,
I may as well go back again.

73

You tell me that you're leaving
Me everything in your will.
Since seeing is believing,
I can't be sure until . . .

LXXV

FESTINAT Polytimus ad puellas;
invitus puerum fatetur Hypnus;
pastas glande natis habet Secundus;
mollis Dindymus est sed esse non vult;
Amphion potuit puella nasci.
Horum delicias superbiamque
et fastus querulos, Avite, malo
quam dotis mihi quinquies ducena.

LXXX

NE laudet dignos, laudat Callistratus omnes.
cui malus est nemo, quis bonus esse potest?

75

A is a runner after girls;
B, grudgingly, behind his curls,
Admits to being a boy; young Z
Has porky buttocks daily fed
With 'mast'; Y's queer, but hates it; X
Could have been born the other sex.
I'd rather put up with these haughty,
Querulous, bloody-minded, naughty
Boys than be married to some bitch
Who makes me miserably rich.

80

Because he hates to praise by name
He praises everybody. Vice
And virtue must look much the same
To one who calls the whole world 'nice'.

XCII

SAEPE rogare soles qualis sim, Prisce, futurus,
si fiam locuples simque repente potens.
Quemquam posse putas mores narrare futuros?
dic mihi, si fias tu leo, qualis eris?

XCIII

QUA moechum ratione basiaret
coram coniuge repperit Labulla.
parvum basiat usque morionem;
hunc multis rapit osculis madentem
moechus protinus et suis repletum
ridenti dominae statim remittit.
Quanto morio maior est maritus!

92

Your question: would my character,
And how, change if I suddenly were
Powerful and rich? Who can foresee
The sort of person he *might* be?
Supposing, Priscus, you became
A lion, would you be fierce or tame?

93

Labulla has worked out a way to kiss
Her lover in her husband's presence. This
Is how she does it. First of all she'll cover
Her pet dwarf with kisses, then her lover
Pounces upon the kiss-beslobbered fool,
Sprays him with further osculatory drool
And hands him back to his smiling mistress. Which
Is the bigger fool – Hubby or Little Tich?

NOTES

BOOK ONE

4. *Caesar*. Domitian. The title 'Caesar' was automatically adopted by emperors.

   Soldiers are free to mock ... Roman troops, following a triumphal procession, were traditionally allowed to shout bawdy jokes and doggerel about their commander, a custom which originated in the belief that this warded off the bad luck which might punish presumption.

   Latinus. A celebrated mime, admired by Domitian.

   Censor. A Roman magistrate, one of whose jobs was the supervision of morals. Domitian had appointed himself to the post for life.

86. A block of flats could be eight storeys high. Martial lived opposite Novius, at the same level, in a narrow street.

87. *Cosmus*. A well-known perfume-seller of the time.

96. *hobbling*. The poem is written in the metre known as *scazons*, literally 'hobbling feet'.

    Baetic. From the region of the river Baetis (Guadalquivir) in Spain.

107. *Maecenas*. Right-hand man of the Emperor Augustus, patron of the arts and benefactor of Horace and Virgil. Died 8 B.C.

     ashes. The Romans cremated their dead.

109. *Catullus' sparrow*. Two of Catullus' most famous poems were about a pet sparrow belonging to his mistress, Lesbia.

117. *Pumice-stone-smoothed and purple-wrapped*. A 'book' was a cylindrical papyrus roll, the ends often smoothed with pumice-stone and the whole brightly wrapped in vellum.

BOOK TWO

36. *Phrygianly short*. In other words, non-existent. The priests of Cybele in Asia Minor shaved the face and head.

    like those defendants sport. Accused men used to appear in court unkempt in order to excite the jury's compassion.

82. In Martial's time slaves still had no legal rights and were in the absolute power of their masters.

NOTES

BOOK THREE

4. *the Aemilian Way*. The road ran from present-day Rimini
to Piacenza.

Forum Cornelii. Now Imola.

the zither. A harpist could make good money in the theatre,
which embraced all sorts of low-brow entertainment.
Compare Book Five, 56.

5. *Marcus Valerius*. Martial's first and second names, the
address normal among friends.

7. Nero had substituted a fixed dole of money, in place of
the traditional gift of a meal, as the patron's payment
for services to his client. Domitian temporarily restored
payment by feeding. If you had a mean patron, as
Martial and his friends point out, you were worse off
than before.

43. *Proserpina*. The goddess of death.

45. *Thyestes*. As an act of revenge, Atreus, King of Argos,
invited his brother Thyestes to a feast and served him
with the flesh of his own sons. Apollo, the sun-god, hid
his face at the sight.

55. *Cosmus*. See note on Book One, 87.

58. *Baian*. Baiae was a fashionable seaside resort.

jars. Wine-jars.

unholy Colchis. Colchis, on the Black Sea, was the legend-
ary home of the witch Medea.

household oil. Oil was used to grease the body for wrestling,
which was for many a daily exercise.

long-haired. Household slaves wore their hair long until
they could do a man's work, when it was cut.

garden god. Priapus. See note on Book Eleven, 18.

60. *The dole's abolished* . . . See note on Book Three, 7.

BOOK FOUR

8. The Roman day, from dawn to dusk, was divided into
twelve hours, varying in length according to the time
of year. Clients attended their patrons in the early
morning, the fifth hour was devoted to the midday meal,
the sixth to the siesta (in summer). Shops opened again
in the afternoon. Martial's divisions are, of course, not
literally exact.

Euphemus. The head of the imperial household.

Ambrosia . . . nectar. The food and drink of the gods: the sort of flattering comparison Domitian encouraged.

sparingly. According to the historian Suetonius, Domitian was a moderate drinker.

64. *the Hesperides.* The fabled gardens of the West.

the Janiculum. A ridge one mile west of the city.

the goddess' wood . . . virgins' blood. The goddess is probably Anna Perenna, an old Latin divinity. The blood probably refers to the virginities lost during the merry-making at the festival.

either road. The Flaminian or the Salarian Way.

Alcinous. In the *Odyssey* the king of the Phaeacians, famous for his beautiful gardens.

Molorchus. A shepherd who gave Hercules hospitality during his Labours and was rewarded with land.

You who now call . . . Most of the smallholdings had given way to large farms run by absentee owners.

66. *Ides or Calends.* Fixed feast-days in each month.

dinner-suit. The *synthesis*, a tunic and small cloak, usually of a bright colour.

knucklebones. Oblongs with two rounded ends, the other four sides being flat, unmarked by numbers but recognizably different. Dice (the same as modern dice) were favoured by the sophisticated. Gambling, though frowned on by the law, was widespread.

BOOK FIVE

10. *the ugly temple.* The temple of Jupiter on the Capitol, damaged by fire and inelegantly restored by Q. Lutatius Catulus in 62 B.C.

Ennius. The 'father of Roman poetry', who first adapted the Greek hexameter to Latin.

Menander. Famous Athenian writer of comedies (342–291 B.C.), whose plays continued to be popular on the Roman stage.

Corinna. The probably fictitious heroine of Ovid's *Amores*.

18. *this month.* December. The Saturnalia, beginning on the seventeenth and lasting for several days, was the most important holiday of the year. Presents were traditionally exchanged.

39. *Hybla.* A Sicilian mountain celebrated for its honey-bees.

The beggar in the Odyssey. Irus.

56. *Grammar or rhetoric.* The primary and secondary main
subjects in Roman education. Grammar consisted of
the study of syntax and literary texts, rhetoric of train-
ing in fluency and logical ingenuity in presenting an
argument.

Tutilius. A now obscure rhetorician of the first century
A.D.

the chorus. In the theatre. Compare Book Three, 4.

74. Pompey's sons, Gnaeus and Sextus, were executed in
Spain and Asia Minor respectively, after continuing to
fight in their father's cause. Pompey himself was
assassinated in Egypt after his defeat by Julius Caesar
at the battle of Pharsalus (48 B.C.). What became of his
dead body is not known.

76. *Mithridates.* King of Pontus, Rome's chief eastern antag-
onist until his defeat by Pompey in 66 B.C. His carefully
built-up immunity to poison is graphically described by
A. E. Housman, *A Shropshire Lad,* LXII.

78. *city of learning.* There was an important university there.

BOOK SIX

17. The man addressed is imagined as a freed slave who had
changed his name to make it more 'Roman'.

45. The Julian Law, enacted by Augustus and revived by
Domitian, laid down severe penalties for adulterous
wives.

46. There were traditionally four chariot-racing factions in the
Circus, each with its loyal fans – the Reds, the Whites,
the Blues and the Greens. (Domitian added the Purples
and the Golds.) Charioteers were frequently bribed.
Domitian did not support the Blues.

BOOK SEVEN

61. Because of traffic congestion, in A.D. 92 an edict of Domi-
tian forbade shopkeepers to encroach on street space with
their stalls.

87. *deadly ichneumon.* This mongoose-like animal is in fact
harmless.

BOOK EIGHT

61. *knobbed.* The cylindrical roll round which the papyrus
(paper) was wrapped was often equipped with decora-

tive knobs at either end. The back of the papyrus was
dyed yellow with cedar oil to preserve it from mould and
moths.

71. *Septicius*. A second-rate silversmith.

BOOK NINE

68. School classes began at dawn and continued till midday.

Thracian. One of the staple entertainments in the amphi-
theatre was combat to the death between a gladiator
with a light shield and a scimitar, known as the 'Thra-
cian', and a more heavily armed opponent.

70. '*Bad times! Bad morals!*' A translation of the often-quoted
'*O tempora! O mores!*' from Cicero's speech against the
revolutionary Catiline in 63 B.C. Catiline's army of the
discontented, including slaves, was crushed by the
government forces soon afterwards.

father and son-in-law. Julius Caesar and Pompey, who had
married Caesar's daughter, Julia. After her death their
precarious alliance collapsed and civil war broke out.

BOOK TEN

8. The point is: the older she is, the better – the sooner he will
benefit from her will.

74. *Scorpus*. According to an inscription this charioteer died
at the age of twenty-seven after 2048 wins.

80. *Murrine cup*. Murrine ware, made from a rare mineral
(jade?) from Parthia, fragile and purple, white or flame-
coloured, fetched huge prices.

90. *Andromache . . . Hecuba*. Hector's wife and mother.

94. *Alcinous*. See note on Book Four, 64.

97. *Myrrh and cinnamon*. Perfumes were thrown on to the
burning pyre by relatives and friends. The ashes were
afterwards collected in an urn and buried in the grave.

BOOK ELEVEN

18. *Diana's wood*. The worship of Diana was associated with
woods, many of which were sacred to her.

the great Calydonian boar. The wild beast which, according
to Homeric legend, the offended goddess Artemis (Diana)
sent to ravage Calydon. It was killed by the king's son,
Meleager, after a great hunt.

the garden god. Priapus, whose crude statue, complete with sickle and erect penis, was carved and placed by farmers to encourage growth.

24. *knights ... senators.* The second and first ranks in the Roman class-structure. Each had a defined range of political duties.

39. *an ex-slave aping Cato.* Charidemus had been freed (a common reward for loyal service) by his old master and promoted to a high post in the household, having previously, as was common practice, acted as 'governess' and tutor to the young heir. The new master, unable to cope with him, compares him to Cato the Elder (234–149 B.C.), whose self-conscious rectitude in carrying out the duties of the office earned him the name of 'the Censor'.

56. Indifference to death and discomfort was one of the tenets of Stoic teaching. In the case of some 'philosophers' this degenerated into a morbid attraction towards suicide and a needlessly squalid style of life.

Nestor. The oldest of the Greeks at the siege of Troy.

73. *left hand.* The hand superstitiously associated with shame and dishonesty.

96. *German.* A slave as a result of having been taken as a prisoner of war.

98. *lictors.* Minor officials, one of whose duties was to precede a magistrate and clear the way, carrying the ancient symbols of authority, a bundle of birch-rods and an axe projecting from them.

curule chair. An ivory folding-seat used by the higher magistrates.

people you don't want to kiss. And therefore, by implication, people who don't want to kiss you.

99. *Symplegades.* The Clashing Rocks through which the Argonauts, in search of the Golden Fleece, had to pass into the Hellespont.

102. *the aediles.* The small body of officials responsible, among other things, for the conduct of religious observances and the reporting of all prodigies.

104. *it's a known fact ...* The evidence for this and the other 'facts' cited is not known.

Ganymede. Jupiter's attractive cup-bearer, who was carried off to heaven by the god disguised as an eagle.

Lucretia. The archetype of the virtuous Roman wife, who

killed herself in shame after being raped in her husband's absence.

Laïs. A celebrated Athenian courtesan of the fifth century B.C.

BOOK TWELVE

18. *Aventine.* The hill on which the temple of Diana stood.

Juvenal. The friend whom Martial is addressing is almost certainly the famous satirist.

cut the youngsters' hair . . . See note to Book Three, 58.

28. *Massa.* Baebius Massa, condemned in A.D. 93 for embezzlement as proconsul of Baetic Spain.

as marvellously as a stag . . . A popular fallacy, shared by the naturalist Pliny.

a unanimous handkerchief. If the majority of the spectators in the amphitheatre waved their handkerchiefs when a defeated gladiator appealed, he might be spared or given a discharge by the Emperor or the presiding magistrate.

bald. Their heads were shaved.

31. *Nausicaa's father.* King Alcinous. See note on Book Four, 64.

34. *divide The days by pebbles.* It was the custom to record days by pebbles, white for happy days, black for unhappy ones.

68. *Poor morning client.* See note on Book Four, 8.

INDEX OF FIRST LINES